Right-Wing Alternative Media

This book offers a fresh perspective on central questions related to right-wing alternative media: Can right-wing media be alternative? Why do they exist? Are they a threat to the existing order and what have the reactions been from mainstream politicians and media actors?

The rise and success of right-wing populism in the political life of many western countries, along with several new and apparently successful alternative media operations on the right, has caused surprise and confusion among researchers and debaters. How should this challenge to mainstream politics and media be understood? Journalistic, political and academic discourse has struggled to explain these tendencies and tends to focus on sensational and extreme examples, with little attention directed towards other aspects. This book critically discusses existing theoretical frameworks related to alternative media in general, analysing a wide scope of cases to illustrate the diversity of voices in alternative media on the right and highlighting the importance of intellectual coolness and common sense in discussions about this important but ideologically and politically charged area.

An important addition to the current discourse of contemporary media, *Right-Wing Alternative Media* is ideal for researchers, students and anyone interested in politics and public discourse.

Kristoffer Holt is Associate Professor at the Department of Mass Media and Communication (MCM), Gulf University for Science and Technology (GUST), Kuwait. His research has focused on the relationship between media and public discourse, especially aspects related to alternative media, religion, ethics and political communication. His work has appeared in the *European Journal of Communication, New Media & Society, Information, Communication & Society, Journal of Mass Media Ethics* and *Media and Communication*, among others.

Communication and Society
Routledge Focus on Communication and Society
Series Editor: James Curran

Routledge Focus on Communication and Society offers both established and early-career academics the flexibility to publish cutting-edge
analysis on topical issues, research on new media or in-depth case
studies within the broad field of media, communication and cultural
studies. Its main concerns are whether the media empower or fail to
empower popular forces in society; media organisations and public
policy; and the political and social consequences of the media.

Bad News from Venezuela
Alan MacLeod

Reporting China on the Rise
Yuan Zeng

Right-Wing Alternative Media
Kristoffer Holt

For more information about this series, please visit: www.routledge.
com/series/SE0130

Right-Wing Alternative Media

Kristoffer Holt

Routledge
Taylor & Francis Group
LONDON AND NEW YORK

First published 2020 by Routledge

2 Park Square, Milton Park, Abingdon, Oxon OX14 4RN
605 Third Avenue, New York, NY 10017

Routledge is an imprint of the Taylor & Francis Group, an informa business

First issued in paperback 2022

Publisher's Note

The publisher has gone to great lengths to ensure the quality of this reprint
but points out that some imperfections in the original copies may be apparent.

British Library Cataloguing-in-Publication Data
A catalogue record for this book is available from the British
Library

Library of Congress Cataloging-in-Publication Data
Names: Holt, Kristoffer, author.
Title: Right-wing alternative media / Kristoffer Holt.
Description: London; New York: Routledge, 2019. |
Series: Communication and society |
Includes bibliographical references and index.
Identifiers: LCCN 2019018932 (print) | LCCN 2019020726 (ebook) |
ISBN 9780429454691 (ebook) | ISBN 9781138318304
(hardback: alk. paper)
Subjects: LCSH: Alternative mass media. | Mass media—
Political aspects. | Conservatism. | Right-wing extremists.
Classification: LCC P96.A44 (ebook) | LCC P96.A44 H65
2019 (print) | DDC 070.1—dc23
LC record available at https://lccn.loc.gov/2019018932

ISBN: 978-1-138-31830-4 (hbk)
ISBN: 978-1-03-233820-0 (pbk)
DOI: 10.4324/9780429454691

Typeset in Times New Roman
by codeMantra

Contents

vi *Contents*

Introduction

On Friday 15 March 2019, a shooter entered two mosques during the Friday prayer in Christchurch, New Zealand: The Al Noor Mosque and the Linwood Mosque. Fifty one people were shot dead and numerous more were wounded. The victims were picked randomly and with no discrimination, even children were gunned down. The shooter, a 28-year-old Australian citizen, acted, in his own words, as a soldier at war to take revenge on the "invaders for the hundreds of thousands of deaths caused by foreign invaders in European lands throughout history." The attack was live streamed through Facebook, using a body camera, and the video was widely circulated, since copies of it kept being uploaded in various social media even after it had been banned. Many mainstream media outlets, like in the UK, MailOnline, the Mirror and The Sun, published edited versions online (but chose to take it down quite soon after publishing it). His preparations before the attack indicate that he aimed to obtain maximum media attention. He published a manifesto that was also made available to the public through the media, either with links to the full text or through summaries of the content. The Christchurch terrorist was soon reported to be a person "marinated" in extremist online culture. He was active on forums like 4chan and 8chan, renowned for unbridled racist and misogynistic meme culture (Nagle, 2017). His manifesto is full of references to the most common tropes of the more extreme right-wing alternative media and online subcultures: The birth rate of whites is declining throughout the world, while the birth rate of immigrants in predominantly white nations is higher, and this will in the future cause a replacement of the white population; Muslims in particular are therefore an existential threat to Europe and other countries hitherto ruled by European descendants; the political elites are contributing to this development and constitute a threat for the future of white children and women. Especially he named Islamist terror-attacks and the number of immigrants who rape white women. He rebukes those men who are passive and do not take action to change the course of history, and he foretells a future in which white men throughout the world will become radicalized and take up arms in order to take back their countries. The purpose of the attack was to create more division and polarization in order to speed up the process.

As if journalists and reporters throughout the world were unable to read between the lines of the terrorist's careful PR management of the attack, many immediately did exactly what he wanted them to do (as clearly indicated in his manifesto): Start quarrels about stricter gun laws and connect the dots between violent far-right extremism, white supremacy and populism in general (and Donald Trump in particular), thereby fuelling the polarization and division that is already present in western countries – exactly as the terrorist wished. And this is, indeed, a sensitive and painful issue in today's debate in many countries. Polarization is largely regarded as one of the most salient problems in modern democracies, since its effects are manifested so obviously through mainstream news reporting as well as in our social media and alternative providers of news and views, and thus not only involving rational disagreement about opinion, but increasingly fuelling unwillingness to compromise (Grafstein, 2018). The terrorist thus cynically exploited both the social media giants and their inability to stop the live stream from spreading as well as the polarized state of public discourse for making his message have maximum impact.

This sinister attack on people, gathered in a house of worship, coincided with the deadline for this book, and, sadly, the events put the topic of it – right-wing alternative media – in a gloomy perspective, because it puts the spotlight on the most extreme cases of alternative media, those which incite to hatred, violence and the destruction of our societies. These clearly exist and must be taken seriously as a phenomenon in its own right. But, on the other hand, what happens when radicalized individuals who find support and encouragement in online spheres where extreme views are promoted and shared commit real acts of terror, it does render them more powerful and influential than they actually are, especially when the news media are so Pavlovianly fascinated with sensational and spectacular events. Having studied the whole spectrum of right-wing alternative media (and especially immigration critical alternative media) for several years, my view is that this is only a small part of the whole story and that failure to acknowledge this only fuels the polarization further. Politicians and activists are often quick in turning such events, committed by twisted individuals, into political points by trying to imply connections between their opponents' views and those of the perpetrator. Journalists, comment-ers and even scholars too often uncritically follow their lead and so-lidify such narratives further. One of the main aims of this book is to offer my insights about right-wing alternative media from a scholarly perspective, while trying to avoid such tendencies as much as possible.

It is easy to get the impression that there are serious problems in the realm of public discourse throughout the western world. Journalism is under pressure, polarization is tearing our cultures and social worlds apart, and public trust in the media as a source of reliable informa-tion is constantly undermined by populist rhetoric – and, to be fair, by declining general quality and lack of impartiality of mainstream journalism. In the US, President Donald Trump has been engaged in a veritable war with the big media houses ever since his campaign was launched to run for president in 2016. CNN reporter Jim Acosta was deprived of his "hard pass" and thus access to the White House press conferences after he refused to leave the microphone during a press conference where he questioned the president's policies. After a judicial decision, Acosta regained his credentials quite soon, and a legal process awaits to determine whether the White House restricted Acosta's freedom of expression. This happened only a week after home-made pipe bombs were sent to CNN's New York editorial by a fanatical Trump supporter with mental problems. As an observer from the outside, watching the major American news networks for just one day leaves one with the impression of a system that is essentially broken. These tendencies, perhaps at present most blatantly visible in American public discourse, are, however, not an isolated phenome-non. Throughout the world, journalism is struggling.

The Washington Post co-worker Jamal Khashoggi, described as a moderate critic of the Saudi regime, was brutally murdered on 2 October 2018, during a visit to the Saudi Embassy in Istanbul, by Saudi agents. At the same time, 319 journalists have been arrested in Turkey since the coup attempt there on 15 July 2016, of which around 180 are still in cus-tody (Turkeypurge.com). In Russia, 58 journalists have been murdered since 1992 (CPJ, 2018). Around the world, many journalists testify of an everyday life where it has become normal with both hateful messages in the inbox and direct threats to their own person. In Sweden, 58% of the country's journalists report that they have at some time been subjected to threats, harassment and violence in their professional role (Nilsson, 2017). In social media there is recurring disinformation and propaganda campaigns with the aim of creating confusion and hostility between different groups – often through links to polarizing and tendentious information or completely false statements (Faris et al., 2017).

There is no doubt that media – in general thought of as a platform for public discourse – is facing challenges today, challenges that will be necessary to deal with also in the future: Distrust and hostility towards media and journalists; "fake news" and propaganda campaigns in social media.[1] These phenomena are, however, problematic to discuss on many levels, especially as the public debate around them tends to be fuelled by indignation and conducted in falsetto – often with more opinion than facts as a basis. What these challenges have in common is that they are, in various ways, an expression of the vulnerability of journalism in a globalized and digitized world. The professionalism and business model of news journalism is challenged; journalist's competence and claim to convey objective/impartial, truthful and relevant information is strongly questioned by many, and individual journalists' safety and freedom to manoeuver is narrowed, often by self-censorship. The harsh political climate also puts journalism's societal monitoring function in an uncomfortable spot. Media actors are increasingly drawn into the game of power and are tempted to become an active party in the ongoing conflicts (Mancini, 2013). This is, again, perhaps most evident in the US, where the big TV companies such as Fox News Network, CNN and MSNBC do not even try to pretend that they are impartial anymore. Instead, news reporting is conducted in the manner of a full-scale war, and for the audience there is no doubt about which side the respective channels are on – which also informs their choice of news (Medders & Metzger, 2018).

Why do I start a book about right-wing alternative media on this note? Simply because this is the setting in which right-wing alternative media tends to be debated. If you allow me to oversimplify for the sake of demonstration, there are mainly two explanatory models for the reasons behind the conundrum western culture, and politics finds itself in at this point: The first one simplistically assumes a priori that mainstream journalism is something good and noble in itself and that its holy mission is threatened and under attack from evil right-wing politicians and alternative media operations (probably in secret collaborating with Russian agents and trolls) who deliberately wants to deceive the public, inflict propaganda and incite to hatred. The other extreme would instead argue that since the mainstream media are just acting as puppets of certain powerful political interests, and mouthpieces of the politically correct ruling class with progressive values, they ignore the real issues of ordinary people and actively try to silence dissenters who criticize them and who speak uncomfortable truths. The growth of alternative media is then seen as a natural, necessary and healthy reaction in response to a corrupt and biased media industry, as a "glitch in the Matrix," as one debater has put it.[2]

Of course, such one-sided descriptions need to be refined, but in general, and to my surprise, these are basically the lines along which the debate can be summarized. There is not much hope for any consensus or progression in terms of mutual understanding here. Against this background, this book is an attempt to summarize what I have learned from doing research about various kinds of right-wing alternative media during the past five years.[3] It has been a difficult book to write, since things keep happening and the media landscape is changing at a rapid pace. I first started taking an interest in immigration critical alternative media in 2014, while doing other research about citizen journalism in Sweden. I noticed a number of blogs, YouTube channels, Facebook pages and pods that all had the same thing in common: Strong opposition towards Sweden's immigration politics and equally strong aversion against the mainstream media, who were described as mainly driven by left-wing/liberal activists who saw it as their job to educate the public to approve of a generous immigration system and to explain away all possible problems related to the high influx of immigrants in Sweden. This was before the migration crisis of 2015, before Donald Trump's unexpected victory in the 2016 presidential election, before Brexit, before the PEGIDA marches in Germany, before the rise of Jair Bolsonaro in Brazil and before the yellow vest protests in France and other countries. The intensity and level of engagement that I observed in the Swedish immigration critical counter movements was apparently not an isolated phenomenon – it turned out to be a manifestation of sentiments held widely in many parts of Europe and the rest of the world. And in all this, various forms of alternative media have played a crucial role.

It is not strange that we today see alternative media that express alternative right-wing views in many parts of the world. We live in turbulent times, and many countries are going through dramatic cultural and demographic changes that affect people's lives at many levels. Immigration is certainly the most pressing issue of the time that dramatically affects and challenges the collective identities of nation states, puts pressure on the welfare systems and sometimes invites to cultural clashes between newcomers and the natives. It is, however, not only the immigration issue that seems to mobilize parts of the public in acts of resistance against what is perceived as a hegemonic system that looks out for the interests of the ruling elite, while forcing rhetoric of a world without borders down the throat of ordinary people who have to suffer the consequences. While focusing mainly on the immigration issue in alternative media, I have also realized that this burning issue is linked to a larger discourse of opposition to a generally "progressive" agenda. Here are some examples of viewpoints frequently voiced in various right-wing alternative media:

Globalization itself, and the social consequences of it (such as decreased sovereignty of nation states and the shipping away of factory jobs to low-wage countries), is questioned as many find themselves as the losers that are sacrificed on the altars of politically correct virtue signalling (and profit for global corporations). Increasingly, and in a similar fashion, resistance against various policy implementations inspired or dictated by gender ideology is causing widespread opposition, and is increasingly a part of right-wing conservative as well as populist discourse (Kováts, 2018). Furthermore, it is not only in Sweden that public service and mainstream commercial news media are written off by many as left-wing propaganda channels, this thought resonates through slogans like "Lügenpresse" in Germany and "Fakenews" in the US. In the UK, the former leader of the UK Independence Party (UKIP), Nigel Farage, has often made a similar case about the BBC and other mainstream media channels. In France, the concept of "Réinformation" has been introduced through alternative media, such as *Novopress*, *Boulevard Voltaire* and *Réinformation TV*, as a strategy of "re-informing" those who, according to them, have been "misinformed" or even "desinformed" by the mainstream media.

The education sector and the universities are also facing these accusations. In Brazil, an important part of Jair Bolsonaro's campaign was the promise to fight the ongoing ideological indoctrination of children in the schools (Romancini & Castillho, 2019). The academic world in general and the humanities and social sciences in particular are in many countries likewise perceived more as breeding grounds for ideas that compete with each other about being most radical and ideologically correct at the same time, rather than as places where it is possible to pursue wisdom and knowledge freely, without the risk of being punished for arriving at the "wrong" conclusions.

What all these things have in common is the idea that the major cultural institutions in society are – in part or wholly – dominated by perspectives that promote left-wing and/or progressive liberal agendas in an oppressing manner that cracks down hard on any dissent, especially through mechanisms of exclusion, such as labelling critics in a way that stigmatizes them (for example, as "xenophobes," "homophobes" and "misogynists"), not allowing controversial speakers to appear at campuses and other forms of actions that are directed at the individual's possibility of making a living (the risk of losing one's job). This is perhaps most prominently visible in the so-called Intellectual Dark Web (Weiss, 2018). This has become an umbrella term for a quite varied group of debaters, academics and intellectuals who primarily seek audiences through social media channels. Figures as diverse as the evolutionary biologist Bret Weinstein, neuroscientist Sam Harris, the comedian Dave Rubin and psychology professor Jordan Peterson are often mentioned as part of this loosely organized network. What unites them is not primarily a common political or ideological agenda, but rather a sense that academic and intellectual freedom is seriously under threat because universities and the media are so influenced by left-wing identity politics and political correctness. Questions like problematic aspects of multiculturalism, the relationship between race and IQ and the fundamental differences between men and women are often pointed out as subjects that cannot be seriously discussed anymore within the realm of the mainstream cultural, political and academic institutions.

Another example of symbolic questions that many express frustration about right-wing alternative media is the "war on Christmas," the changing of traditions in various places around Christmas or renaming of the holiday in order to accommodate groups who presumably could take offense with events with such clearly Christian background. In my view, it is important to keep this in mind when discussing alternative media, since it says something important about the way many people feel about the cultural and intellectual climate of today, they can be described as reactions against different perceived "deficits of the so-called progressive actors" (Kováts, 2018).

As a media scholar, it is not my job to say if those who feel the way I just described are right or wrong in their analysis. Personally, I agree with some of the views I come across in my empirical material and disagree with other things. But my professional aim is to try and understand how their acts of expressing these views through media affect the surrounding media landscape, and as a consequence, society as a whole. News outlets like *Breitbart News* in the US, *Fria Tider* in Sweden and *Junge Freiheit* in Germany are very interesting as media phenomena, and studying them can tell us much about the present world of media as a whole. In order to do that, it is also necessary to understand why people choose to dedicate time to express such views publicly, what it means to them, what it means to their audiences and how it relates to the larger picture of other media channels in society. In my view, this is important to point out and as you will see later in this book, I argue that one of the problems in research about alternative media hitherto has been an unfortunate tendency to assume normatively determined qualities of "good" and "bad" about specific types of alternative media and to analyse cases accordingly. If alternative media (of any persuasion) is good or bad is to me a secondary question, the primary reason why they are interesting is simply because they exist, have an audience and are meaningful in many people's lives.

Right-wing?

I have been reluctant to use the phrase "right-wing." This is because it is a somewhat misleading and at times confusing label. As sociologists Kathleen M. Blee and Kimberly A. Creasap put it: "There is little uniformity in how scholars characterize the right in modern Western societies" (Blee & Creasap, 2010, p. 270). They also point out an important observation that right-wing movements are usually "known for what they are against, not for what they support" (p. 272), a point often also made elegantly many times by conservative philosopher Sir Roger Scruton about conservatism (Scruton, 2002). The pro-life movement, for example, is usually counted as a right-wing movement, but it arose as a response to the emergence of legal abortions and the violation of the sanctity of life that was sanctioned by this. Sometimes, "right-wing" is used about groups that cannot be called merely conservative, but are, so to speak further to the right and therefore carry connotations of extremism (Blee & Creasap, 2010). As such, it is also clearly and outspokenly something that many scholars who have studied it deem negative and that needs to be countered. In an anthology about "Right-wing women," for example, the editors start by stating: "We hope this book contributes to increased understandings of and debates on the scope and importance of right-wing women and furthers anti-right-wing practice" (Bacchetta & Power, 2003, p. 1), an attitude that is, it can be argued, questionable from an academic perspective, but nevertheless widespread. Other times, right-wing implies a much broader spectrum and simply means any position that opposes "progressive" liberal or left-wing positions such as gender ideology and high taxes to fund public spending on social causes.

What complicates things even more is that even if we construe right-wing as a position that is to be defined according to what it is against (as implied above), they might be very much against other phenomena that are also considered right-wing. For example, it is clear that the alternative media that we are talking about here often are critical of groups and people who traditionally would be assumed as representatives of the more moderate political "right." Populists, as well as many alternative media, target the global capitalist elites, and there are many expressions of frustration with the apparent weakness of more traditional mainstream conservative movements, like the Republican party in the US (the insult "Cuckservative" is a much debated example of this, see Rappeport, 2015).

Paternotte and Kuhar highlight this tendency and cautions against lumping together:

> ... phenomena as diverse as populism, far right parties, religious fundamentalism, nationalism, racism, neoliberalism or austerity politics. These are often gathered under the broad umbrella term of 'Global Right', which identifies right-wing actors in opposition to the advocates of progressive causes.
>
> (Paternotte & Kuhar, 2018, p. 7)

The authors make an important point about the study of such counter movements that is similar to the one I am trying to make in this book about alternative media, and they should get credit for it. Scholars, they argue,

> ... should rather engage, (...), with the complexity of these oppositional dynamics and be careful about the concepts they use. This implies fine-grained theoretical and empirical work to better understand what is exactly at stake, as well as meticulous comparative research not to overstate what could be context-specific.
>
> (p. 17)

This imperative is commendable, but it also highlights the sometimes very difficult task of being nuanced and context-sensitive, while at the same time trying to say something that will be of relevance even outside of specific contexts. In order to point out that there are indeed differences among the various positions that are included a bit sloppily under the term the "global right," you still need to invoke the notion of the global right. And this is precisely what I mean when I talk about "right-wing" alternative media. The way I see it, the label right-wing can be used as an umbrella term – so long as it is acknowledged as such, and that there is a clear realization that the more extreme variants that might be squeezed in under that umbrella are not used to smear the others that are also standing under it. One of the best attempts to summarize what the conflicts between left and right are about is the way it is put by Wesley McDonald in the *International Encyclopedia of the Social Sciences*:

> For nearly two centuries, these competing groups battled each other mostly over questions of economics and class. The Right defended the propertied interests of the privileged classes while the

Left sought to equalize wealth and property. For the most part, they debated the extent to which wealth should be redistributed through government intervention. In the early-twenty-first century, cultural and social issues, such as abortion, same-sex marriage, secularism, and multiculturalism, have come to play a more dominant role in Left-Right political struggles.

(p. 248)

As a response to such a development, researchers in political science have proposed the additional notion of GAL/TAN – Green Alternative, Liberal vs. Traditional, Authoritarian, Nationalist (Hooghe, Marks, & Wilson, 2002). While being useful in the sense that it points out other dimensions than merely the difference in economic concerns, and points to other causes of division, like the climate, nationalism and traditional values, the right/left division remains a central division and one that is needed in order to make sense of contemporary politics (Jahn, 2011). Importantly, what, I think, makes this relevant to study is the very notion of "alternative" in combination with "right-wing" – an aspect that will be developed in the next chapter.

Notes

1 I will discuss the problematic aspects of the expression "fake news" later in this book.
2 This phrase is used by journalist David Fuller in a YouTube documentary about the Intellectual Dark Web on his channel *Rebel Wisdom*.
3 The different parts of the different chapters therefore mainly represent ideas and findings that I have also presented in my previously published works.

1   Why do alternative media exist?

Can right-wing media really be "alternative"? My answer is yes, of course. The definition used in this book is one that I have developed in a recent article together with Tine Figenschou and Lena Frischlich. In our opinion, alternative media should be considered primarily as (*self-*) *perceived correctives* of "'traditional', 'legacy' or 'mainstream' news media in a given socio-cultural and historical context" (Holt, Figenshou, & Frischlich, 2019). The definition reads like this:

> Alternative news media represent a proclaimed and/or (self-) perceived corrective, opposing the overall tendency of public discourse emanating from what is perceived as the dominant mainstream media in a given system. This stated "alternativeness" can emerge on and should be studied on multiple different levels: Alternative news media can publish different voices (alternative content creators) trying to influence public opinion according to an agenda that is perceived by their promoters and/or audiences as underrepresented, ostracized or otherwise marginalized in mainstream news media, alternative accounts and interpretations of political and social events (alternative news content), rely on alternative publishing routines via alternative media organizations and/or through channels outside and unsupported by the major networks and newspapers in an alternative media system.
> Such an umbrella definition takes a relational approach as a point of departure. In other words, the alternative quality of any news medium is derived from claims to its counter-or complementary position to certain hegemony, since this must be construed as the organizing principle behind alternative media enterprises.
> (Holt, Figenshou, & Frischlich, 2019)

The primary interest is not to determine who is actually entitled to name themselves "counter hegemonic" – instead the important thing is being able to define and study a phenomenon that is increasingly widespread and relevant to public discourse in our time: "Media of different positions that promise to oppose what they see as dominant, influential and agenda setting news media that shape the worldviews of citizens in a ways that they don't agree with and therefore seek to counter" (Holt, Figenshou, & Frischlich, 2019). And these can, of course, be found on the left as well as on the right.

Right-wing alternative media that express criticism of immigration have made an audible impact on public discourse in many countries. We can see the same tendencies in Europe, the US and Brazil (Aalberg, Esser, Reinemann, Strömback, & De Vreese, 2016). In Germany, Alternative for Germany (AfD) labels the established media the "Pinocchio press" (Binder, 2015). In Austria, the Freedom Party (FPÖ) has complained multiple times against the public service station Österreichischer Rundfunk (ORF.) Although we perceive massive mistrust in traditional media by politicians inside and outside Europe, the connection between these movements and the established media is more complex, since every political movement is dependent on publicity (Mazzoleni, 2008) – and vice versa, the media feed on the spectacularism of populist politicians such as Trump, and the constant novelty of scandal, controversy and surprise (Lawrence & Boydstun, 2017).

How do partisan alternative media affect the surrounding media landscape? It is clear that they have become important players in the realm of opinion formation and the cultural debate (Holt, 2017; Nagle, 2017). Expressions of distrust and hard-hitting criticism towards mainstream media are frequently voiced throughout Europe and the US. The claim is that hegemonic mainstream media withhold or thwart the reporting on information that can be sensitive in light of a politically correct agenda. In Sweden a number of debaters of different political leanings who are critical of Sweden's comparatively very generous immigration politics and its consequences to parties such as the Sweden Democrats (SD) routinely utter criticism along these lines, although their approaches vary greatly (Holt, 2016a). They voice media skepticism, distrust and criticism in what could be called immigration critical counter-publics (Downey & Fenton, 2003; Leung & Lee, 2014) in Sweden. Similar phenomena are visible throughout the western world.

It is, however, also clear that the scholarly (as well as mainstream journalistic and political) reactions to the appearance on the scene of phenomena such as the so-called "alt-right" online movement and other, more moderate examples such as the blog *Ledarsidorna.se* in Sweden, have been marked by outrage as well as surprise and confusion. This confusion is perhaps best illustrated by the example of how Canadian psychology professor Jordan B. Peterson has been labelled "alt-right" by some debaters (Lynskey, 2018). As a phenomenon, Peterson is highly interesting, and some of the outrage coming from politicians, academia as well as media illustrates this. Peterson gained fame, mainly through YouTube, after publicly protesting against the Canadian government's Bill C-16, which would require the use of "preferred pronouns" when addressing people with trans-identities. In Peterson's view, this is nothing but "compelled speech," which goes against the logic of allowing freedom of speech to citizens in democratic countries. He has been described as a far-right agitator, and his insistence on the scientifically obvious psychological differences between women and men in the face of gender theorists famously caused Sweden's feminist Foreign Minister Margot Wallström to comment "Climb back under your rock!", after his visit to Sweden in November 2018 (The Local, 2018, November 8). From the scholarly perspective, Peterson has faced resistance from colleagues at his own university (petitions were signed to oust him from his tenure position), as well as a number of other scholars who take issue with his views on gender as well as his harsh criticism of postmodernism and Marxism (Bartlett, 2018). How can a university professor who merely expresses his views on a new law, holds lectures about the bible and publishes self-help books that resonate with a lot of people (mostly, it seems, young men) be associated with far-right extremism, the nebulous "alt-right" and even white supremacy? Anyone who has listened to his lectures will find such claims absurd, but still, many regard his popularity as a threat to democracy, and as a symptom that dark forces are about to take over the planet.

This confusion has partly to do with a mismatch between the dominant theories about alternative media, on the one hand, and of reality, on the other. Scholarly work about alternative media has in essence taken its cue from Gramsci and the concept of hegemony. Alternative media from that perspective is construed as a liberating force of empowerment for groups who are otherwise marginalized in public discourse. The expression "mainstream media" has a clearly left-wing origin and has been mostly used by radical scholars like Noam Chomsky. Researchers who have studied media and activism often describe alternative media in idealized terms, almost as an expression of the ideal type of plebeian or subaltern public formation (see, for example, Atton, 2015; Bailey, Cammaerts, & Carpentier, 2007; Lievrouw, 2011; Pajnik & Downing, 2008). Most researchers, with exceptions (see, for example, Atkinson & Leon Berg, 2012; Rauch, 2015), have therefore focused on cases such as the Occupy Wall Street movement and their activist use of alternative media (Penney & Dadas, 2014). Few, if any researchers, conceptualize right-wing resistance against elitist and politically correct mainstream media according to such narratives.

This illustrates the need for viewing opposing media channels, especially online participatory media in the light of their position as a *self-perceived* correctives of traditional mainstream media. These media present alternative interpretations of political and social events and try to influence public opinion according to an agenda that is often mainly critical of, for example, immigration politics and the perceived threat of Islamization of western countries – although the main focus and level of impact on the system (Capoccia, 2002) varies greatly between different actors. While some are extreme and violent, others are moderate and reasonable. The aim is to analyze how these attempts succeed and in what ways they manage to create an impact on public discourse. It is necessary to nuance the discussion of how alternative media (especially with ideological/political agendas that clash with predominant values of the mainstream media) affect public discourse. The main point is that I introduce an important theoretical distinction between different types of anti-systemness ("ideological anti-systemness" and "relational anti-systemness" – see Chapter 2). This theoretical framework is applicable to any alternative media, regardless of their political orientation.

Given the predominantly "progressive" qualities ascribed to counter-hegemonic alternative media in much previous research, it seems that many scholars are reluctant to use the term alternative media about right-wing cases, and instead employ terms like "junk news," "fake news," "hyper partisan media," "conspiracy media" and "propaganda outlets" (see, for example, Hedman, Sivnert, & Howard, 2018). While acknowledging that these terms might accurately describe some problematic phenomena in today's highly polarized and combative media environment, I argue that "alternative media" is a valid description of media on the right as well as on the left (or, any other movement that employs media for counter-hegemonic purposes, for example, religious or cultural). According to my stipulation, alternative media are run by various kinds of actors who publish alternative reports and interpretations of current events as a direct response to the perception that the perspective they promote (political, ideological, moral, cultural and religious) is being unfairly treated in the mainstream media. In that sense, they are first and foremost "reactive" (Haller & Holt, 2018) and always exist in an oppositional relation to what is perceived as the mainstream. While it is likely that this definition will include many examples of false reporting, propaganda,

extremism, hate speech and a high level of partisanship, these qualities cannot be assumed from the outset, but must instead be demonstrated through careful research in cases where such descriptions are
appropriate (Holt & de la Brosse, 2017; Holt, Haller, & de la Brosse,
2019). Alternative media might also exhibit various levels of (positive
or negative) impact on the surrounding media landscape and associated public discourse. While many alternative media who promote extreme or fringe agendas probably "live their lives mostly unnoticed by
the vast majority" (Holt, 2018, p. 55), other more moderate alternative
media may manage to attract a large following and also reactions from
the mainstream media that put them in the spotlight. In my view, it is
therefore important, from a scholarly perspective, to study both the
alternative media on the fringes and more moderate alternative media
and their relation, interaction with and impact on the wider public
discourse. In order to address the emergence of what in this book is
called "right wing alternative media," we need to continue by making
some additional introductory definitional work.

The question why alternative media exist in the first place is intimately related to the question of how we define alternative media. Let
us examine the existing definitions further. As stated above, the definition of alternative media is, in turn, also intricately tied to the question
of what it is supposed to be an alternative to "mainstream media,"
a concept that also needs to be looked at, especially in the light of
some common uses of this term. Alternative media has been defined
in different ways throughout the history of scholarship on media.
Historically, the phrase "mainstream media" has been used mostly
by left-wing debaters, such as Noam Chomsky (1997), and by media
scholars, "alternative media" has long been considered the embodiment of a dream about giving ordinary citizens a way of speaking back
to power (See for example: Atton, 2015; Bailey et al., 2007; Lievrouw,
2011; Pajnik & Downing, 2008). Most researchers have therefore focused on cases such as the Occupy Wall Street movement and their activist use of media (Penney & Dadas, 2014). There has been an evident
reluctance by researchers to talk about far-right activists or right-wing
populist criticism of the "politically correct" and "leftist" mainstream
media using existing theoretical frameworks. Typically, the theoretical frameworks that have guided most research since the 1970s are
derived from a critical analysis of mainstream media and the idea of
a needed alternative that operates beyond the control of it as a vehicle
for oppositional voices. A kind of critical perspective on media that
perhaps most apparently occurred in academic and intellectual circles
has often sprung from or been inspired by clearly left-wing thinkers
like Antonio Gramsci, Theodor Adorno and Stuart Hall.

In left-wing thought, this critical view of mass media is of course related to the notion of hegemony. Hegemony is maintained, according to Gramsci (1992), a lot because intellectuals in various ways represent the interests of the ruling class and explain reality to the subjects in such a way that they experience the power relationships as self-evident or as commonsensical, and therefore give their consent to letting themselves be governed. The media are seen as a central arena for the ruling class to seduce the population into a passivating "false consciousness." The historian of ideas Thomas Bates (1975) has captured the core of Gramsci's conceptualization of hegemony:

> Civil society is the marketplace of ideas, where intellectuals enter as "salesmen" of contending cultures. The intellectuals succeed in creating hegemony to the extent that they extend the worldview of the rulers to the ruled, and thereby secure the "free" consent of the masses to the law and order of the land. To the extent that the intellectuals fail to create hegemony, the ruling class falls back on the state's coercive apparatus which disciplines those who do not "consent," and which is "constructed for all society in anticipation of moments of crisis of command ... when spontaneous consensus declines.
>
> (Bates, 1975, p. 353)

In order to rule a country, it is not enough with simply a monopoly of violence along with clear sanctions for the violation of laws. There must be a superstructure that is carried by cultural institutions such as schools, newspapers and churches, which in various ways cooperate in a kind of apologetic project to give people in a society sufficiently good arguments for them to keep calm and not protest against experienced injustice or abuse of power. It is thus an analysis that is largely based on a mistrust of the elite in society and the institutions that represent them. The way that news media are portrayed is here characterized in such a perspective by both cynicism and mistrust. The explosive stuff in Gramsci's texts is of course the strategy he then develops to successfully break the hegemony and replace it with another. It is not possible to change society only with a revolution – it requires a "long march" (Marcuse, 2014) through the institutions of society and culture, where it is crucial that the "right" people end up in the right positions and that a new form of narrative about the state of affairs comes in place and is implemented from above.

Ideas, and not only material conditions, play a central role in all social change that will have a chance to succeed. Much of the left-wing critical discussion about the media's role in society has therefore often dealt with barriers to or opportunities for social change by changing, for example, concepts and descriptions of reality used in the media. From this point of view, alternative media have always been regarded as a way to counteract the establishment in a political as well as cultural way and pave the way for a new order, as the traditional media have been construed as conservative counter forces in the process of social change. Criticism has focused on the role of the media in the maintenance of a mass culture that aims to legitimize the capitalist system. In the *Alternative Media Handbook* from 2007, for example, alternative media is defined in the following way:

> 'Alternative media' are media produced by the socially, culturally and politically excluded: they are always independently run and often community-focused, ranging from pirate radio to activist publications, from digital video experiments to radical work on the Web.
>
> (Coyer, Dowmunt, & Fountain, 2007)

The quote is a very good example that echoes what could be described almost as a scholarly consensus about the nature of alternative media – it is the embodiment of a vision of empowerment of those who in different ways and to various degrees are being marginalized, misrepresented and ostracized by mainstream media. James Curran's foreword to the book is also a very good illustration of the most common scholarly construals of alternative media as a phenomenon that enables:

> ... divergent social groups to define and constitute themselves, facilitate internal strategic debate, and further the forceful transmission of their concerns and viewpoints to a wider public. The engaged media of working- class groups; the feminist movement; sexual minorities; ethnic minorities; peace, environmentalist and anti- global poverty groups; and others, have all extended the diversity of the media system, and enabled grassroots voices to be better heard.
>
> (p. xvi)

It is clear from such a description that the need for alternative media comes from the fact that mainstream media, the most important channels for news, debate, entertainment and culture in a given country, behave in a way that does not accommodate various groups' perspectives and interests in a satisfactory manner. Therefore, alternative media serve the purpose of accommodating such groups and interests as mentioned in the quote above.

This kind of definition goes back to a longer tradition of thinking about radicalism, activism and opposition to mainstream media's representation of reality as being oppressive, stereotyping and reinforcing commonly held prejudices and the "status quo" (Shoemaker, 1984). While there is an apparent opposition between media scholars with a liberal-pluralist view and those with a critical Marxist view about media's role in society, most scholarly work on alternative media stems from the latter. Marxist criticism of capitalist societies holds that mainstream media's role is crucial for the "class-based nature of those societies ... that serve to bring about and to maintain ruling class domination and exploitation" (Mullen & Klaehn, p. 2016). There are, of course, variations in this tradition, some are more focused on the economical and ownership aspects of media while others focus more on identity and representation (cultural studies much inspired by Stuart Hall). One of the most radical media critics during the last 50 years has been Noam Chomsky, who describes the American mainstream media as ideological instruments which represent special interests of power and privilege. As institutions, they are, according to Herman and Chomsky's propaganda model, based on the exercise of power and domination within society that inevitably affects the way they chose what topics to cover and how (Chomsky, 1997; Herman & Chomsky, 1988). The propaganda model argued that the most influential sources for news (the elite media) tended to report in a way that fosters "consent" for the decisions and interests of the societal elites. Chomsky talks about the mainstream media as an integrated part of the power structure in society:

> They are way up at the top of the power structure of the private economy which is a very tyrannical structure. Corporations are basically tyrannies, hierarchic, controlled from above. If you don't like what they are doing you get out. The major media are just part of that system. What about their institutional setting? Well, that's more or less the same. What they interact with and relate to is other major power centers – the government, other corporations, or the universities. Because the media are a doctrinal system they interact closely with the universities.
>
> (Chomsky, 1997, p. 2)

Indeed, this dictum has a conspiratorial ring to it, and the Herman and Chomsky propaganda model has received heavy criticism from within the field of media and communication studies (Mullen, 2010). Neverthe-less, this way of thinking about mainstream and alternative media is to some extent the characteristic of most research about alternative media. An influential early study that incorporated the notion of alternative media was presented by Negt and Kluge in 1972. Their ideas take Jürgen Habermas' (1989) theory about the bourgeois public sphere as starting point, and envision a "proletarian" alternative public sphere that would constitute a counter-power to the organized interests of the bourgeois public sphere by its potential to organize resistance, a " counter-publicity against the bourgeois public sphere" (Negt & Kluge, 1972). In their highly reverential analysis of the book in the journal *New German Critique*, Knödler-Bunte, Lennox, and Lennox (1975) described the Marxist and revolutionary underpinnings of their work: "Negt and Kluge's book thus attacks the fatal division of labor which separates narrowly specialized academic investigation from a revolutionary political theory directed to-wards praxis" (p. 52). Negt and Kluge's work has been cited by numerous authors since its publication, and part of the appeal for many scholars seems to be precisely the ambition to unite a radical aim with the enter-prise of research – a tendency that this is still very visible in today's com-munity of scholars interested in activism and alternative media.

In a similar vein, although not citing Negt and Kluge, Nancy Fraser (1990) criticized Jürgen Habermas for similar reasons, proposing the need to take into account the notion of "subaltern counterpublics," constituted by groups of people who for various reasons are not on "participatory parity" with more privileged groups, and hence lack the realistic possibility of making their voices heard in a bourgeois version of deliberative democracy, since the system would always be rigged against them. Alternative media is in this view seen as a vessel for the disadvantaged to make their voices heard, to resist the hegem-onic societal discourse and to "speak truth to power."

In recent years, however, this kind of "left wing romanticism" (Downey & Fenton, 2003) or "academic idealizations" (Holt, Figenschou, & Frischlich, 2019) of alternative media has been slightly revised in different ways. The alternative/mainstream dichotomy have been described more in terms of a scale rather than as closed off and separate categories (Atton 2002a, 2002b, 2015; Atton & Wickenden, 2005; Downing, 2003; Hackett & Gurleyen, 2015; Kenix, 2011; Rauch, 2007). This is especially relevant in the context of an online public sphere, where distinctions between journalism and other fields such as PR are increasingly difficult to point out. Also, the possibly inhibiting aspects of the lack of professional journalistic training and competence as well as vulnerable economic plans and scarcity of technological knowledge in alternative media are the issues that have been raised (Atton, 2002a, Doudaki, Carpentier, & Christidis, 2015). Also, the alleged grass roots quality of alternative media has been problematized, since it has been shown that alternative media are often not purely run by idealists, but also by platforms where elite activists and organizations operate (Atton & Wickenden, 2005; Holt & Karlsson, 2014). Also, it is today problematic to talk about the supposedly oppressive qualities of mainstream media without taking into account those who voice such views the loudest today – right-wing populist politicians rather than marginalized minority groups.

Media criticism today

When we look at the expressions of media distrust that have become so common and widespread today (the view of the media companies and its employees as corrupt and the establishment's mouthpieces and spokesmen) it is remarkable that this kind of rhetoric is so reminiscent of the kind of mistrust of the "bourgeois" media that have come from the left side so often. For example, have a taste from these quotes, which are fresh examples of how media distrust is expressed on various Swedish immigration critical alternative media. The first example is a quote by Vavra Súk, the editor in chief of Swedish far-right weekly newspaper *Nya Tider (New Times)*:

> The establishment's media scandalize people so they lose jobs, friends, education and may be forced to move from their homes. (…) This is in principle affecting exclusively regime critics or those who deviate from the corridor of opinion.
>
> (Súk, 2017)

Here, the public disciplination of dissenting thinkers is highlighted as an important factor in how the mainstream media collaborates with rulers to maintain hegemony. Throughout right-wing alternative media in different countries, similar claims are made routinely and are stated more as a matter of fact than a question for further investigation. Another quote from *Infowars* clearly illustrates the same kind of thinking:

> Government and the mainstream media have lost all credibility, leaving opportunity for the alternative media to swoop in and expose the truth, waking up people across the globe.
>
> (Wilson, 2013)

The message is that mainstream media deliberately favor some perspectives and frame news by withholding information in order to control people's opinions and that they have a deliberately skewed selection when it comes to letting people with different opinions be heard. This in turn leads to the feeling that the democratic system does not work properly as there are built-in barriers to free exchange of views in the public conversation and that important information is retained. This thought figure, of course, is not only found in alternative media but is also widely used in political contexts. Jimmie Åkesson like Donald Trump, Marine le Pen and Geert Wilders have in principle expressed the same thing. The German PEGIDA movement has also made this kind of criticism a main issue (Haller & Holt, 2018). This analysis holds that the rulers in society are represented by an intellectual/cultural/political and media elite that defends the current order, rather than questioning those in power and holding them accountable. The reason people do not protest is that they are in fact in a state of false consciousness. In short, people are fooled, naive and blue-eyed, and in the hands of a corrupt elite who cares more about maintaining their own positions than about how common people are doing.

Criticism or distrust?

It is important to distinguish between ideologically motivated and strategically formulated mistrust against the mainstream media – and the intellectual elite holding the power over the interpretation and description of reality, on the one hand, and those who simply experience genuine uncertainty about whether news in general are reliable sources of information, complete and free from consideration of who may benefit from the way some problems are being described. It is not possible to equal the expressions of media distrust I illustrated above and an underlying right-wing agenda. Those who put forward that kind of criticism differ too much from each other for it to be possible to connect them all into a common ideological core, while at the same time the media criticism they publish is quite consistent and similar (Holt, 2016a). Here we get into what really is the difference between media criticism and media distrust. As it is impossible to guarantee the perfect covering of all events and circumstances in society, an ongoing and open media-critical discussion is needed about how the media succeed in presenting news to the public in a way that enables a democratic system of well-informed citizens (Holt & von Krogh, 2010). If many people find that journalists do not do their job properly, but allow half-truths, consciously frame issues to benefit their own purposes or to avoid uncomfortable issues, we can say that the criticism causes media distrust or is an expression thereof.[1] We can see examples and a tendency of distrust in the Swedish debate on how immigration issues have been addressed (Truedson, 2017). But here it is important to keep criticism and distrust separate. When distrust is motivated by an experienced ideological underdog position and the strategy to tackle that underdog position involves undermining general trust in the media, we are immediately transferred from the arena of critical discussion to the arena of ideological cultural struggle or "metapolitics" (see Chapter 3) – and this is a veritable minefield because the stakes are so high.

Also, it is not at all unthinkable that the critique presented even with such starting points can also be based on true, or partially true, observations (see, for example, Lundell, 2008). In the Swedish case, for instance, many would agree today that there actually were some truth in the criticism levelled at the mainstream journalist before 2015 by immigration critical alternative media of very different ideological positions: Questions related to problematic aspects of immigration were largely off the table for reporting, and certainly not encouraged by politicians or influential editors (Truedson, 2016). Therefore, criticism in itself cannot be assumed a priori as irrelevant or as merely malicious propaganda with ideological motives. Having said this, the accusations and criticisms in alternative media are many times exaggerated, speculative and often discredited their opponents on unfair grounds, while actually pointing out real problems on other occasions. Here we end up in a bog that is difficult to navigate for many. This becomes clear in the debate about whether the media covers up problematic immigration-related issues or not (Truedson, 2016). On the one hand, it can be argued that some problems have been underreported and some questions have not been asked as they should. These are legitimate critical questions that can also be linked to and discussed based on empirical observations. On the other hand, in the expression "cover-up" there is an intentionality that is always assumed and attributed to those accused of doing the covering up. Often, such criticism is based on assumptions about underlying motives that are difficult to measure or investigate. It is often here that the ideological dimension becomes visible. Here is an example, taken from a comment posted on the identitarian blog Motpol.se, criticizing public service for seeking out and doxing anonymous critics of the health-care system in Sweden:

> Swedish Television's outspokenly hostile "investigative report"
> at the same time confirms something many predicted already
> when immigration critics began to get visits by journalists in their

homes and publicly shamed in the media, this is a slippery slope and the same methods would eventually be used against other uncomfortable critics.

(Andersson, 2017)

Here, the point of departure is clearly that the journalists who conducted the investigative report had a malicious agenda from the outset, and that the purpose of reporting is interpreted as a form of disciplination of dissenters. This form of distrust can be compared to other examples where more concrete things constitute the substance. A commonly occurring point where the Swedish established media is criticized is the one that deals with immigration's long-term costs (Holt, 2016a). This is a type of question that can actually be discussed in a fairly reasonable way. It is possible to study how journalistic texts are designed. It is possible to reason about the actual costs and how to calculate. Comparisons can be made and then critically discussed. This is a completely different kind of criticism, and the distrust that may be derived from such a discussion is of a different nature compared to that which is derived from the assumptions of intentions and motives behind a perceived bias in the reporting. However, in the heat of polemics, these types are often mixed together, which does not favor a constructive discussion.

It is also important to remember that mistrust per se is necessarily subjective. Whether or not the accusations are true, they represent personal experience that something is not right. Of course, this does not mean that biased framing never occurs (because it certainly does), but it tells us that the experience of scope and direction (who is being disadvantaged by the framing) is often not as obvious as we think. Because distrust is subjective in this way, it does not really matter if there is a reason to believe it or not, it still affects people. As pointed out by Walter Lippmann, it is primarily "the pictures in our heads" that are important for humans to organize their lives (Lippmann, 1922) – the experience or the picture that something in a certain way has consequences even if it does not match actual conditions. The fact that people distrust the media's reporting about certain subjects is enough for us to start asking questions about why. In such a discussion, it is not enough to dismiss it as only the result of malicious ideological propaganda or metapolitical efforts. Then you risk losing important aspects and sweeping problems under the carpet. The discussion must also be open to the fact that criticism can be linked to a legitimate criticism and justified questions.

Media criticism is not new or unique to our times; it has been present since (at least) Socrates critique of the written word (Nehamas, 1988).

But such attitudes are perhaps voiced today more vociferously and powerfully than before through alternative media – and with higher stakes, since such narratives almost unavoidably are tangled up in ideological/political struggles. During his election campaign, Donald Trump made the criticism of "mainstream media," or with another term "fake news media" (Trump [realDonaldTrump], 2018), into a main part in his often conflict-oriented style. It was obviously a successful strategy. Trump expressed feelings towards the established journalism that many, especially Republican, electoral groups agree with. Exactly how many are difficult to say (51% of Republican voters agree on Trump's description of "fake news media" as "the enemy of the people," see Malloy & Rubenstien, 2018). During his time as president, this attitude toward, in particular, CNN, but also other established and influential news agents such as *The Washington Post* and *The New York Times*, has been demonstrated almost daily. And the emotions are answered – both during the election campaign (Patterson, 2016) and after the election (Patterson, 2017), reporting has been predominantly massive and negative about Trump on all major news releases in the US, with Fox News as the only exception (although initially predominantly negative there too but with a small margin).

While many journalists seem to dislike Trump's politics, they seem to love to write about him – which puts the Trump-critical journalists in a problematic situation as they both give him free attention while delivering their criticism – and suddenly the journalist himself is a part in the matter, a player on the field that they are reporting on in a way that is not completely compatible with how journalism is usually described (Gutsche, 2018). And the criticism in itself can also have an opposite effect than the one intended:

> … Fairly clear evidence that many Trump voters are the same voters who reject the legitimacy of the mainstream press, it is doubtful that his mainstream media coverage influenced his electoral success – except by reinforcing these voters' notions about press bias …
>
> (Lawrence & Boydstun, 2017, p. 152)

Here we can see a clear challenge for journalism today and most likely tomorrow. Distrust of media is not an isolated phenomenon, it is widespread around the world. In Germany, representatives of Alternative Für Deutschland (AfD) call the news journalism for "Pinocchio-press" (Haller & Holt, 2018). There are various ways to explain this phenomenon. One explanation could be that mainstream or legacy media journalists have really done a bad job and actually represent a left-wing liberal elite that lacks contact with large groups of ordinary people's perception of which issues are important and which systematically frames news to promote their own perspective at the expense of others (Major, 2015). This is an issue that is relevant to discuss and an option that must be kept open. Another explanation is the "Hostile Media" effect (Vallone, Ross, & Lepper, 1985) which shows that representatives of different opposing interest groups tend to perceive exactly the same news report as unfairly biased towards their own group. When people are exposed to media content that is perceived as unfavorable to their own group, a natural reaction seems to be questioning its credibility:

> Group members, concerned with the perceived inaccuracy of the portrayals and convinced that the portrayals undermine the group's legitimacy in the larger society, cope with derogating media coverage, viewing it as hostile biased.
>
> (Perloff, 2015, p. 10)

However, such an explanation does not give the whole picture, as it does not take into account whether the actual news reporting in question is generally fair or, in fact, contains angles and insinuations or omissions which can be seen as expressions of a biased position. What it does show is that it is probably very difficult to get people who already have an aversion and suspicious attitude towards the established journalistic channels to change their attitude. Research also shows that such attitudes can motivate people to actively try to counteract the influence that the perceived inaccurate news reporting can entail, by making their own voice heard publicly (Barnidge & Rojas, 2014). This can be expressed in alternative media initiatives.

Counter-publics, Hallin's spheres and the "corridor of opinion"

The notion of counter-publics is useful for understanding the dynamics of today's media landscape, and becomes crucial in relation to the whole dichotomy between alternative and mainstream media (Fenton, 2008; Leung & Lee, 2014). Strikingly, theories about the formation of online counter-publics have been designed mostly to work on "progressive" cases while the most interesting developments that this term captures today appear to be related to various right-wing, "alt-light," populist or radical "alt-right" phenomena. The phrase "corridor of opinion" was coined by political scientist Henrik Ekengren Oscarsson in 2013 in a blog post about Swedish political culture (Hallin, 1989; Oscarsson, 2013). It is related to Hallin's (1989) notion of different spheres for public discourse (the sphere of consensus, the sphere of legitimate controversy and the sphere of deviance). This notion will be relevant in Chapter 3, as it captures a claim often made by those critical of mainstream media (MSM) and active in alternative media: That some things are impossible to say, some standpoints are immediately ruled out as illegitimate or deviant by the general discourse in the mainstream. This in turn hampers free debate and puts a lid on relevant discussions (in Sweden, this is most often applied to the debate about immigration, where an anti-immigration standpoint for long has been described as belonging outside of the "corridor of opinion" or in Hallin's terms, in the sphere of deviance).

* * *

In this chapter I have tried to go through explanations for the existence of alternative media: By doing so, I also believe that I have been able to provide a good definition of what I mean by the problematic prefix "right-wing" as well as with the contested notion of "alternative media." Importantly, I have argued that right-wing alternative media need to be addressed as any other kind of alternative media – as the result of the fact that some people choose to act on their experience of representing some perspective that is perceived as treated unfairly in the mainstream media. As such, it is obvious that the existence of alternative media is related to the increasingly polarized political climate that we find ourselves in today. But it must also be remembered that polarization is by necessity caused by the existence of two opposing poles. In my view, alternative media are for the most part "reactive" (Haller & Holt, 2018), or "relational" (Holt, Figenschou, & Frischlich, 2019), in the sense that they act in relation to something that is already there. The alternative needs an original in order to have something to be an alternative to in the first place. Just like populist politicians gain popularity through articulating (and perhaps also fueling) many people's disappointment in and distrust of the mainstream media as well as the political establishment, alternative media are fuelled (and perhaps also fuels) by the same sentiments. The point is that those sentiments are in some sense organic. We can argue about the accuracy or inaccuracy of describing CNN as "fake news" or the Swedish public service TV as a tool for left-wing propaganda, but even in the unlikely case it would be possible to demonstrate that

CNN is in fact always objective and fair in its reporting, and that left-wing bias almost never affects the framing of news in Swedish public service radio and TV, it would not make much difference, those who feel this way would most likely not change their opinion.

Note

1 By Yariv Tsfati defined as: "The feeling that journalists are not fair or objective in their reports about society and that they do not always tell the whole story" and that journalists "will sacrifice accuracy and precision for personal and commercial gains" (Tsfat, 2003, p. 67).

2   Are alternative media a threat to the system?

Donald Trump's victory in the American presidential election 2016 left many wondering what mistakes were made in the many analyses that had almost unanimously predicted a win for Hillary Clinton.[1] In the subsequent discussions, many attempts were made to explain what had gone wrong. One explanation has seemed to gain the most support: The rift between the powerful elites and ordinary, common people must have grown so big that the elites no longer understand how the grass roots think, and what problems are important to them. In the US, journalists were shocked that Trump's rhetoric targeting "fake news media" was attractive to a large number of people (Barbaro, 2016). At the same time, "fake news" and "disinformation" has often been held up as one of the explanations for why Trump won (Blake, 2018). Journalists also had to realize that alternative news sites such as *Breitbart News* had a bigger audience than they had expected even though they were widely described as extreme or representatives of the "alt-right" (Gourarie, 2016) and that they themselves as journalists were regarded by many as part of the corrupt establishment and as politically correct mouthpieces of those previously in power and not as the people's advocates, as scrutinizers of the mighty.

A commonality that many on the right share – conservative or neo-conservative, populist of extreme-right – is a distrust in the mainstream media. The reporting in the major and most influential media channels is often considered to be left-wing biased and yet in bed with the elites of society. Right-wing alternative media, often with a focus on criticism of liberal immigration politics and a harsh tone against MSM, has become an important factor in public discourse in many western countries. We see the same tendencies in Europe, the US and Brazil (Aalberg, Esser, Reinemann, Strömback, & de Vreese, 2016). In Germany leaders of the right-wing populist party, Alternative for Germany (AfD), call the established media the "Pinocchio press"

(Binder, 2015). In Austria, the Freedom Party (FPÖ) have complained multiple times against the public service station ORF. Although we perceive massive mistrust in traditional media by politicians inside and outside Europe, the connection between these movements and the established media is more complex since every political movement is dependent on publicity (Mazzoleni, 2008) – and vice versa, the media feed on the spectacularism of populist politicians such as Trump, and the constant novelty of scandal, controversy and surprise (Lawrence & Boydstun, 2017). And indeed, the academic (as well as the journalistic) reactions to the rapid emergence of such things as the so-called "alt-right" online movement have been characterized by both surprise and confusion, as mentioned earlier in this book (Gourarie, 2016).

I argue that theoretical assumptions about alternative media must be valid regardless of what ideological orientation they have in order to be useful. It is also necessary to view opposing media channels, especially online participatory media in the light of their position as self-perceived correctives of traditional mainstream media. These media present alternative interpretations of political and social events and in the Swedish scene mainly try to influence public opinion according to an agenda that is often critical of immigration politics and the perceived threat of Islamization of western countries – although main focus and level of "anti-systemness" (Capoccia, 2002) varies greatly between different actors. While some are extreme and violent, others are moderate and reasonable (Holt, 2016a). While some are outspokenly anti-system some are not, but may still have a polarizing effect on the media landscape and others yet may show no signs of anti-systemness. Therefore, it would be beneficial to further the discussion of how alternative media with views that are mostly rejected in the discourse of the most important mainstream media impacts on public discourse. One way of doing this is by making a distinction between different types of anti-systemness ("ideological anti-systemness" and "relational anti-systemness" – see Capoccia, 2002; Holt, 2018). This typology is intended to be applicable also to other alternative media, regardless of their ideological/political orientation (Holt, 2016a). Furthermore, this framework is important because it allows for a focused discussion about specific cases and facilitates the distinction between alternative media that do and do not qualify as anti-system. This distinction is extra important since there is a clear tendency among many today, especially among politicians and journalists, but also researchers, to assume or imply a priori that alternative media, especially with a right-wing leaning, poses a threat to democracy (See, for example,

Lewis, 2018). This is, however, somewhat of a simplification that risks obscuring the issue, rather than shedding light on it. Media criticism is certainly not a threat to the system or malicious in itself. Public and critical debates about media are instead something that is often regarded as a sign of a healthy media climate. However, if certain groups in society choose to abstain from participation in the regular mainstream platforms of public discourse (which are normally considered as the common space in society, the "agora") and instead entrench themselves in counter-publics where discourses of alienation and mistrust in conventional democratic channels are fostered and amplified, it can be problematic from a democratic perspective (Kobayashi & Ikeda, 2009; Sunstein, 2007). First, it reveals that some people feel that they cannot participate on equal terms and choose alternative platforms outside the conventional news providers. Second, it can become an obstacle for any form of deliberation between conflicting parts, which in turn poses a challenge for the democratic system (Bossetta, 2012; Fenton, 2008).

In Sweden, support for the Sweden Democrats (SD) was until quite recently much lower than for similar parties in other Scandinavian countries. In the 2010 election, they got into parliament, and their support has grown remarkably since then (from 5.7% in 2010 to 17.5% in 2018 and in some recent polls around 20%). During this time, much media coverage has been devoted to various scandals related to the party and its members. The party has, like many other populist politicians and parties, successfully presented themselves as victims of an unfair media bias in the mediated political debates (Hellström & Nilsson, 2010). They claim that the mainstream media has silenced debate about immigration and has ostracized critical opinions (see Holt, 2016a; Rydgren, 2005). Rhetorically, this has worked very well for SD, since much criticism of the party has been easily explained away with references to "media bias." A number of incidents also surfaced during 2015 and in the early 2016 (i.e. the debate about media and police cover-ups of sexual harassment and abuse of young women during the "We are Stockholm" festivals in 2014 and 2015) that to many seem to confirm such a claim. Especially after the ruling Social Democratic Party all of a sudden decided to take measures in order to radically lower the amount of asylum seekers during the 2015 migrant crisis, even established journalists have argued that there is truth to the claim that immigration has been off limits for serious discussion in the Swedish public sphere due to the stigma of alleged racism (Truedson, 2016).

If massively negative media coverage in the mainstream channels has not hampered the increasing support for SD, it may be because there are other voices available which play an important and perhaps underestimated role in public discourse. There are indications that right-wing alternative media in Sweden have a reach (especially in terms of causing reactions on social media) that in some cases can be compared to some of the biggest mainstream media outlets (Borgs, 2015; Newman, Fletcher, Kalogeropoulos, Levy, & Kleis Nielsen, 2018). These alternative media are often depicted in mainstream media as a threat to the free society and as cesspools of hatred and lies. While there might be truth in such claims in several occasions, the problem is that the immigration critical alternative media tend to be lumped together and treated as a unified whole and often attributed with connotations of extremism. In particular, the anti-mainstream media rhetoric is targeted and described as problematic and a threat to free-dom of speech. Again, some actors actually do threat and target indi-vidual journalists while others tend to publish more critical opinions and analysis that cannot be characterized as hateful or threatening. Examples like this make it important to make distinctions that allow us to see the differences between alternative media that can be said to have anti-system tendencies and those who do not. Being critical of mainstream news is not the same thing as promoting extreme agen-das or the infringement of media freedom. Furthermore, it could be argued that when references to "media bias" can be used effectively to brush off criticism, it is probably because many agree about the gen-eral analysis. Such attitudes are crucial to understand from a scholarly perspective: Why are people with the "Lügenpresse" or and in turn how this may affect public discourse on a general level. Are they a threat to the democratic system and is their existence a danger to free public discourse? If so, in what ways?

The reason why right-wing alternative media is relevant to study is that their existence and ways of acting can have an impact on and change the conditions for public discourse. A constructive approach to the study of this field can handle distinctions between specific al-ternative media (regardless of their specific views) while at the same time recognizing the variety. In an attempt to accomplish this, theo-ries about anti-system parties (Capoccia, 2002) can be useful. When a new and ideologically controversial party wins support, the political dynamics are affected in certain ways. Likewise, when new media that promote standpoints considered by others as intolerable enter the arena and win an audience, the surrounding media are most likely affected by this. If these media, like some parties, can represent positions that are harshly critical of the political establishment and the elites and at the same time express opinions that are very far from other actors in the arena, some specific problems arise. The effect of such changes is often described as increasing political polarization, and the legitimacy of the established political system is challenged (Sartori, 2005). Media that can be described in similar ways (anti-establishment rhetoric, undermining confidence in the current order and positions far from the rest of the media actors) contribute to increased polarization in the public debate conducted through media in a society. Also, among right-wing alternative media, we can see that there are major differences in how the various actors relate and position themselves to other media actors and to what extent their legitimacy is challenged (Holt, 2016a). Therefore, it is necessary to distinguish between the different types of anti-systemness in a more elaborated manner.

Different types of anti-systemness

As stated above, these media channels need to be analysed against the background of their self-positioning as correctives of traditional media and of constrained public discourse. Such attitudes can occur both to the left and to the right, and Capoccia (2002, drawing on Sartori, 2005) distinguishes between *relational anti-systemness* (how the party positions itself in relation to other parties and vice versa) and *ideological anti-systemness* (whether or not the ideological foundation of the party includes an agenda to alter or destroy the system). It is thereby possible to discuss different types of "anti-systemness" and to widen the definition beyond strictly anti-democratic movements. Many European parties in the category that Mudde (2014) calls "populist radical right parties (PRRPs)," for example, cannot be considered ideologically anti-democratic, but can still show signs of *relational* "anti systemness," placing them in the category "polarizing parties" according to Capoccia (2002). This distinction in regards to anti-systemness is relevant to make also in the sphere of alternative media. Right-wing alternative media position themselves as contenders or rebels against established media's norms and ways of working (for example, ethical codes stipulating caution when reporting on crimes committed by immigrants) in which the mainstream media is understood as the mouthpiece of the political establishment, rather than the watchdogs of the politicians. As a response to this, various actors – of a wide range of positions – have created a number of alternative media that present different interpretations of reality, and may report in a way that is considered unorthodox by journalists in the mainstream. This is cause for studying if they show signs of anti-systemness and in what ways. These media, like anti-system parties, display anti-system characteristics to various degrees and for various reasons: Some are clearly

RELATIONAL ANTI-SYSTEMNESS

		YES	NO
IDEOLOGICAL ANTI-SYSTEMNESS	YES	Anti-system Alternative Media	Irrelevant Alternative Media
	NO	Polarizing Alternative Media	Not Anti-system Media

Figure 2.1 Typology of anti-systemness in relation to traditional media's positions, norms and ways of working, taken from Holt (2018), based on Capoccia (2002).

anti-system in their ideological positionings visible in the content they publish, while others who are not still appear to be anti-system in the relational sense (See Figure 2.1) because of the polarizing dynamics that are set in motion in relation to other media outlets. Furthermore, some alternative media might not show any signs of anti-systemness, relational or ideological, which is also important to keep in mind.

Ideological anti-systemness

Ideological anti-systemness refers to the degree of hostility and distrust displayed by the specific alternative media towards mainstream media and their institutions within the established media system of a nation. Capoccia (2002) explains Sartori's definition of ideological anti-systemness as adhering to a belief system that "does not share the values of the political order within which it operates" (Capoccia, 2002, p. 14). In other words, it is a stance that would remove the whole system of governance rather than merely challenging and opposing those who happen to be in power at the moment. Obviously, this represents a quite extreme position and would entail a vision of a completely different media system. Ideological anti-systemness can be studied through self-descriptions, interviews and content analysis of material available through the specific alternative media (blog posts, pods, articles, YouTube clips, etc.). In order to fulfil this criteria, it must be clear that the view taken on mainstream media is clearly antagonistic and excludes any hope for change or remedy of the perceived ills.

One example of such an outspoken position in the Swedish case, which can be found in Holt (2016), is an interview study with activists in Swedish immigration critical alternative media: The now defunct YouTube channel, *Granskning Sverige*, that specialized in regularly interviewing journalists and politicians in a provocative and confrontative manner and recorded the interviews secretly in order to publish them (often in an edited version) displays signs of ideological anti-systemness. The channel generally attacked and targeted mainstream journalists and described the whole media system as rotten and in need of removal and replacement.

Relational anti-systemness, on the other hand, refers to media that may, but do not necessarily, meet the requirements for ideological anti-systemness, but still have an effect on other media. Capoccia (2002) outlines three attributes of relational anti-systemness:

- "Distant spatial location from neighboring parties" (meaning that their views are far from even those who could be described as closest to them). This in turn leads to
- "Low coalitional potential", which in turn tends to entail
- "Outbidding propaganda tactics/delegitimizing messages" (p. 14)

As for parties, these three dimensions are applicable to alternative media: Although they are not ideologically anti-system, they may have an impeding and/or polarizing effect on the media environment as a whole (or, perhaps rather function as media manifestations of a polarizing dynamic already in play in society at large), similar to the effect some parties have on the party system when other actors position themselves strongly against them, for example, through a "cordon sanitaire" or by refusing to participate in the same public debates because their views are considered unacceptable. They can also have the effect that their conduct can change or erode the standards for what is considered acceptable, especially if there is a high demand for the type of content offered through the alternative media. In the Swedish case, the unique selling point of the immigration critical alternative media is in several cases that they provide information about the ethnicity of criminal offenders while this information is generally omitted in the mainstream news. If this type of content is attractive to readers, and hence constitutes a serious competitive advantage for the alternative media in question in relation to mainstream media, it might lead to altered praxis in the mainstream. Such an effect is here deemed the outcome of relational anti-systemness because it would be an effect caused by the fact that other media adapt to new conditions imposed by the mere existence and success of the new actor. (In a long-term perspective, however, if such a development takes place on a large scale, it would cease to be controversial and consequently also lose its anti-system quality).

By putting these two dimensions of anti-systemness in a four-square figure, a framework appears that makes it possible to separate different alternative media from each other based on observations about the applicability of the both notions. If a specific alternative medium displays signs of ideological as well as relational anti-systemness, we can talk about anti-system alternative media as in the upper left square in Figure 2.1. They position themselves (ideologically) in direct opposition to the traditional media standards and functioning (for example, by deliberately not joining the National Press Club, the media ethical system, and by displaying antagonism towards mainstream media actors). Relationally, they also have a direct impact on the surrounding media landscape because other actors openly renounce them (polarization), which often entails a lot of coverage in the mainstream media. The content is of such a nature that it (a) represents a real competitive factor for the mainstream media and (b) could be problematic to publish within the framework of mainstream media publishing channels because of its controversial nature. The combination of (a) and (b) means a theoretical possibility that they may also affect the behavior of traditional media, by, for example, changing practices to avoid losing readers (Cf. Holt, 2018).

Irrelevant right-wing alternative media

If only the criteria of ideological anti-systemness is fulfilled and not the relational (as in the upper left square in Figure 2.1), they can rightfully be described as radical, hostile and antagonistic, but since they are generally ignored by audiences and other media outlets, they might be described as "Irrelevant alternative media," because they simply do not cause publicity and in effect reactions that will lead to any influence beyond the narrow circle of supporters. They are not relationally anti-system in the sense that they have no direct impact on the surrounding media landscape. These are essentially ignored by the established media and are not seen as competition. Their content would be problematic to publish within the framework of the traditional media publishing channels due to their controversial nature. This category includes various blogs, social media accounts and other alternative media outlets run by marginal or fringe groups or individuals who simply do not cause any counter reactions in the surrounding media environment.

A good example is the Swedish PEGIDA movement's Facebook page. PEGIDA is an abbreviation for the German "Patriotische Europäer gegen die Islamisierung des Abendlandes" ("Patriotic Europeans against the Islamization of the Occident"). In the end of 2014 PEGIDA emerged as a protest movement against the political establishment and of increased Islamic influence in Europe. The group gathered for "Monday Demonstrations" in the city of Dresden and they had their peak in the fall of 2015, when they attracted nearly 20,000 protesters one Monday. The Monday Demonstrations soon became more and more radical and infamous in Germany and were widely reported in other countries, and PEGIDA groups were formed in other European countries such as Sweden, Norway, Great Britain or Austria. However, these groups did not transform into mass movements like in Germany. Having done some content analysis of the original German-speaking PEGIDA movement's Facebook page in Germany and Austria (Haller & Holt, 2018), a comparison with the branches that popped up in smaller countries revealed some interesting differences (Holt & Haller, 2017). In Germany, PEGIDA's Facebook page has a substantial following and the movements activities have caused much debate and attracted prime time media coverage worldwide, but the Swedish branch has very few followers and has hardly been noted at all by other media actors, and the interactions on the rare posts appearing on the page are virtually non-existent. The Swedish PEGIDA page is also more oriented towards communication directly with supporters than the German mother page, for example, with information about a planned rally or about the leadership of the movement or with direct calls for actions (such as 'share this post'). The Swedish PEGIDA page also contains significantly lower numbers of links to content in mainstream media than the German counterpart, and instead more links to other right-wing alternative media (Haller & Holt, 2018). The content is also of a more extreme and hateful nature than the German version, with, for example, more images and videos depicting Muslims in a hostile and vulgar manner (Holt & Haller, 2016).

Polarizing right-wing alternative media

Alternative media outlets that are not ideologically anti-system but have attributes of relational anti-systemness could be described as "Polarizing alternative media." They cannot be said to be ideologically opposed to the basic rules and guidelines that govern the established media's approach. They do not express a wish to destroy and replace the whole system, but rather push for alterations and improvements of the existing system. Representatives would not have problems connecting to media-ethical structures or common accountability functions and could actively seek membership in press clubs and journalist associations. However, in order to be placed in this category, the content must be of such a nature that it (1) constitutes a competitive challenge for segments of the mainstream media, and (2) would be problematic to publish within the framework of the traditional media publishing channels – for example, by focusing on controversial subjects that tend to be avoided by mainstream media or depending on the fact that the interpretation and application of the ethical guidelines are different from the traditional media. Relationally, polarizing alternative media might affect the surrounding media landscape in a similar way as the anti-system alternative media – through mutual and outspoken antagonism (an example is that they might not be accepted as members in press clubs, because the "distant spatial location" is considered too great by pre-existing members) and by the fact that these also could theoretically affect other media's behavior.

Right-wing alternative media

The lower right corner of the table is a residual category for alternative media that does not meet any of the criteria for anti-systemness. This category is important in the context of discussing alternative media with agendas that are deemed as provocative and even harmful by some, but do not qualify for the notion of anti-systemness.

The typology outlined above is useful both for selecting relevant cases and for the analysis of them. It will especially be of interest to look specifically at purely "Anti-system" alternative media, with a potency to have a real impact on public discourse and "polarizing alternative media," who might not pose a threat to the existing system per se, but still affect the debate by polarizing it and presenting alternative agendas and interpretations of events that differ from what is generally found in mainstream media to such an extent that meaningful discussions are difficult. Both types from the left column can theoretically also have an impact on traditional media's behavior (see Holt, 2016b). The "Irrelevant alternative media" can be represented by numerous blogs and sites that present views that are radically anti-system, but which do not cause any reactions from other actors nor pose any threat to the power over how reality is described or competition for readers.

Such sites exist in abundance but fail to have any notable impact. In the next chapter I will apply this to a number of actual cases in order to illustrate the usefulness further.

Note

1 This chapter is based on an article previously published in the journal *Media and Communication*: Holt, K. (2018). Alternative media and the notion of anti-systemness: Towards an analytical framework. *Media and Communication, 6* (4), 49–57. doi: 10.17645/mac.v6i4.1467.

3 Right-wing alternative media in research

Having spent the book so far on concepts and discussions about the issue at hand, I will now proceed to discuss right-wing alternative media from a more empirical perspective. Let me start this chapter by presenting a short summary of an interview study that I did in 2016 with some of the most important figures active in the Swedish immigration critical alternative media scene (Holt, 2016a). In the study, I focused especially on asking the respondents about their motives for being active in this type of enterprise, their view of mainstream media and finally how they view themselves in relation to the surrounding media landscape. The results are, in my view, very revealing and open up for a good continued discussion about what can be said about right-wing alternative media more generally from a research horizon.

Motives

At the heart of all the stories the respondents told me about their motivation for engaging themselves in producing content for immigration critical alternative media, there is a fundamental analysis of the Swedish public conversation which is described as limited and controlled by a narrow "opinion corridor." When talking about an opinion corridor, it specifically concerns immigration issues and issues related to Islam (a couple of respondents also mentioned gender and LGBTQ issues, as well as the climate issue, but the central issue is clearly that of immigration). The term "opinion corridor" is widely used by virtually all interviewees. This phrase was coined by political science professor Henrik Ekengren Oscarsson in a blog post in 2011 and has become widely used in public discourse. He defined it as "the buffer zone where you can still voice your opinion without immediately having to receive a diagnosis of your mental condition" (Oscarsson, 2013, my translation). A recurring theme in the interviews was various forms of attempts to get articles published in the established media or comments in the comment field connected to articles. After having been repeatedly rejected or blocked from the comment field, they turned to other publishing channels such as blogs or to start their own newspapers. Sweden is also emphasized as a country that differs from other countries in this respect. It is described as different because it has so "very extreme media," as one interviewed put it. The mainstream media is described as politically correct and as operating within a very narrow opinion corridor. In short, this means that the scope for deviant opinions, or facts that could support them, is very limited and that the persons who represent such views publicly must count on the risk of different types of retaliation. For example, hit pieces in the media targeting people with the wrong opinions are given as examples and – or as a consequence of being publicly shamed in the media – sanctions in the form of, for example, loss of employment, denial of membership in trade unions or problems with families and relatives who become suspicious. This is linked to the power of the media to define what is considered inside or outside the view corridor of opinion and the possibility of hanging out people defined as "outside" in an unfavorable way. But the attitude towards the opinion corridor varies. Overall, I could distinguish between three different approaches.

Eternal outsiders

The first one is when the interview person described their efforts as mainly focusing on "preaching to the choir," that is, creating and maintaining a platform for the voices and perspectives that they experience do not get space in ordinary media. This is an expression of a sense that it is not even possible to change the dynamics of public discourse in a way that would ever tolerate the standpoints they want to express. For this reason, the primary motive is not to convince opponents or reason with them. This position does not entail focusing on reaching out and influencing public opinion at large, as it is perceived as unfeasible. Rather, the strategy is to build a long-term cultural acceptance of one's own world view within a certain circle. This attitude shows that the intended audience is primarily sought among people who are already suspicious of the mainstream media and the political establishment, and the purpose of creating and disseminating content is primarily to offer material that can strengthen and further develop an already critical attitude towards, for example, immigration policy, Islam and the political and media establishment. It signals a certain resignation to the possibilities of having their own views ever tolerated within a larger public conversation within the framework of the large media and therefore created their own platforms outside, something we could call "counter-public." This "isolationist" attitude was only expressed clearly by those interviewed whose ideological leanings could clearly be placed on the extreme or far-right end of the spectrum.

Legitimacy seekers

The second approach does not presume exclusion as their fate, but instead seeks to actively influence a larger spectrum of people and tries to work for legitimizing views that they see as unfairly being ostracized and labelled with negative epithets. It could be described more as an aim of widening the opinion corridor so that there is room for a broader spectrum of views. Here it is a clearly expressed conviction that there is a need for voices in the public conversation that challenges the establishment. The motive for working in alternative media is described as wanting to create counter images to the ones being painted in the established media and of responding to statements and opinions that are expressed there are erroneous. The respondents whose approaches could be placed in this category typically emphasize the importance of having a social debate on immigration that is based on a correct description of reality, based on rational considerations and unrestricted facts, whether it is uncomfortable or not. This is also something that they clearly do not think the mainstream journalists handle very well. Mainstream journalists are described as amateurs who mainly write tendentious descriptions of everything related to immigration, without providing facts and reason.

Entrepreneurs

The third category of motives based on approaches towards the perceived opinion corridor is more entrepreneurial and less concerned with ideals about public discourse. The respondents in this category talk about their alternative media platforms as entrepreneurial projects, where the motive behind primarily lies in the fact that there is a market for the type of news and perspectives they publish there. Underlying their involvement is the basic analysis that there is an audience out there which is under-served by the established media channels due to the opinion corridor. The aim is to offer a product that is missing in the country and whose type of content and perspective they see that there is demand for. The purpose is therefore not primarily, according to the respondents, to influence an opinion with a message or to strengthen the already convinced in their opinions, but rather to take advantage of a market in which there is a demand but not much supply. Of course, this does not exclude the fact that there might also be a will to influence, but it is not stated as the main motive. The goal of running the sites is primarily to achieve profitability.

Based on these three approaches that I could see among the interviewed, it is clear that the input values differ somewhat between the different actors and that the motives, as well as the ideological starting points, shift. While some of the respondents stated a social conservative stances, others expressed a more accentuated nationalist focus – "Swedish-friendly," others expressed identitarian or fascist sympathies. Another category described themselves as libertarians and yet others merely as conservatives and even one social democrat. It is thus difficult, based on the material in this study, to link immigration critical alternative media to a specific motive or some particular ideology, as there is so much difference between the different participants in the study. What unites them is the critical stance on immigration policy, and how the debate and reporting on this is conducted in the established media.

Views on the established journalistic media

The views on and the relationship with the established media expressed by the interviewed were intimately linked to both the motives for the activity presented above and the view of what alternative media are. One could say that a clear common central point in the universe of alternative media is the omniscience of the established media and their ways of acting in that premise. The interviewees also all, paradoxically, admitted that they are largely dependent on "old media" to have material to write about themselves. In a way, they see it to some extent as part of their jobs to read mainstream media, so that the audience do not have to. As some of my other studies have shown, a large part of the content in these alternative media consists of re-writes of material from mainstream media, and the dependence on "old media" has been commented on by several. They are not only dependent on the established media for matter, but also, the very reason they see for themselves to exist, is to counter much of what is written in the mainstream media. One example is that several of the interviewees themselves publish information about criminals' ethnicity when this information is lacking in the established journalistic media reporting.

At the same time, a clear difference between different interviewees lies precisely in the attitude towards "old media." The clear dependence is seen as unproblematic by some and as a natural part of their own positioning. Others stated it as somewhat problematic and expressed as a goal to invest more in self-produced material. These also saw it as a problem that the level of ambition among many alternative media was often low in the past and that it is necessary to embrace the methods of professional journalism (to some extent) in the future. In the long term, here we can see an ambition to be an "alternative" that could be comparable to established media. However, how far they are willing to go varies. Some do not see any problem, for example, in applying for press support, like mainstream newspapers do, in order to exist financially, while others (especially those who identify as libertarians) do not want to apply for principal reasons, and instead rely on income from subscription content on the site or advertising revenue. While a couple state that they are voluntarily affiliated to the press ethical system and have responsible publishers, others choose to stay out of it because they do not trust they will be treated fairly. The reason for not joining the press system is primarily that the ethical guidelines are perceived as "fuzzy" and interpreted in a way that would usually disadvantage their own activities.

None of the respondents currently see themselves as comparable "alternatives" to the mainstream media, but rather as complementary media whose function is to oppose and offer alternatives to the established media coverage and discussion in specific areas. Criticism of the established media is prominent in all interviewees, and there are recurring points, in principle always (with some exceptions) related to how different aspects of immigration (both immigration and its consequences as critics of it) are portrayed.

When the interviewees told me about what they are specifically critical of in the established media, several points were addressed in virtually all interviews. The clearest example they give is that established media (both privately owned and public services) deliberately avoids reporting on problematic aspects of immigration or that they strongly distort the image of what consequences it entails. The fact that Swedish journalists in this way ignore the principle of "consequence neutrality" is something most interviewees mention. Several examples that have been mentioned are about rapes committed by immigrants but where the men should have been described in the media as "Swedes" – something that is attributed to the fact that the journalists are worried that telling the truth would spark hatred towards immigrants. Other examples are about how statistics and facts are deliberately presented

in misleading ways. A recurring flaw, according to most of the interviewed, is that journalists deliberately lay out smoke screens around
issues such as the long-term costs of immigration or the crime rates
of immigrants. With the interviewees (with a few exceptions), there
was no doubt that cover-ups, factual inaccuracy and boycott of certain
voices are being done deliberately and for ideological reasons. They
believe that Swedish journalists believe that some information may
affect people's perception in the "wrong" direction. Another recurring theme is reflections on the fact that the vast majority of Swedish
journalists have clear left-wing sympathies. Here, renowned media
scholar Kent Asp's studies are often cited, which showed that Swedish
journalists' party sympathies in 2011 were clearly left-dominated (Asp,
2012). The general impression is that the image of the Swedish mainstream media is deeply rooted – it is an image that the interviewees
perceive to be confirmed on virtually daily basis and the prospect of
change is not seen as particularly promising. Mistrust of the media
also leads to a feeling that democracy is not working properly as the
public conversation is hampered.

How do they relate to each other?

One of the problems in the debate about the Swedish alternative media has been that the concept itself has not been specified in terms of
which actors are involved and which ones do not. It is often unclear
in the debate which media are meant and how these in turn relate to
each other. Often it talks about alternative media as a uniform concept, which we have not really seen as how those who represent them
look at themselves. Therefore, I asked the interviewees about how they
viewed the concept of alternative media and how they relate to other
actors that are usually included in the same concept.

There is an apparent duality in the answers. On the one hand, it is
stated that the very concept of "alternative media" has become rea-
sonably established and acts as a kind of "brand" or collective concept
for media outlets with content and perspectives that cannot be found
in the established media. In this way, the concept has become useful.
At the same time there are also the reservations. One clear feature of
the interviewees is that they often do not want to be lumped together
with other alternative media. All respondents emphasize the importance of assessing each actor individually. According to what they
have answered, there is in principle no formal cooperation between the
players. Some have connections to each other, and some sometimes

use each other's materials. They do not want to be responsible for what someone else does on their site, or for what visitors on the site/ blog write in the comment fields. Several other alternative media are mentioned that the interviewees (with a few exceptions) clearly do not want to be equated with: Those who are clearly and outspokenly Nazi sympathies, like Nordfront.se. These have ideological profiles that belong to a "different sphere" than the one they see themselves in. For the interviewees, this is an important nuance. They are very upset by a tendency to describe all alternative media as simply sewer pipes of "hate speech" in order to dismiss the claims and criticisms that come from them by equating everyone with the worst examples. It is also clear that they profile themselves in different ways towards each other, both publicity and rhetorical. Some of them, in different ways, strive to imitate the established journalistic media in working methods, layouts and by producing own material and actively trying to become more "professional." What appears can be summarized as follows:

1   Motivation and input values. We can see that the people who were interviewed differ in terms of both the ideological position and the view of what is the goal of the engagement. It is clear that everyone does not argue based on the same strategy – some focus more on reaching a group already have similar viewpoints, while others actively try to drive public opinion and convince opponents and people who are undecided. A third category has as its stated goal to exploit a market for perspectives, opinions and news where there has previously been a void in the established media.

2   Relationship to established journalistic media. Alternative media cannot exist without the established journalistic media as a constant reference point. They define themselves in the light of what they see as their opposite. They are dependent on commenting or writing about material from established journalistic media and reacting to the current news agenda. They do not see themselves as a realistic or comprehensive "alternatives" to the established media, but mainly focus on publishing material and opinions in specific areas where they find that the usual media is erring or just not reporting. The starting point is that the established media do not do their job, deliberately withhold or distort the facts from the public in order to control people's opinions and have a skewed selection when it comes to allowing people with different opinions to speak.

3   How they look at other alternative media. The approach is characterized by duality. On the one hand, the concept of alternative

media has become useful as a "brand," but, on the other hand, there is a tendency to distance itself from other actors who are usually included in the concept, because these represent behaviors and opinions that one does not want to be associated with. A certain tendency towards competition between different actors can be discerned.

The reason why alternative media are interesting to study is that their existence and working methods can influence the public conversation and the surrounding media landscape and thus the conditions for debate and exchange of ideas and news consumption. A starting point for the study has therefore been that the analysis should be able to help us differentiate different actors in a meaningful way. In this case, the analysis aims to shed light on how representatives of different alternative media look at the traditional media, other alternative media and the public conversation at large. Against the background of what has emerged in this study, we can reason about alternative media as a new element in the media landscape and ask questions about how we should understand their possible impact.

Similar to how a country's political landscape is affected when a new controversial party gains mandate, a media landscape, as proposed in Chapter 3, is probably affected when new media enter the arena and win an audience. If these media, just as some parties can do, represent positions that are explicitly critical of the political establishment and social affinity and at the same time express opinions that are very far from other actors in the arena, some specific problems arise. Just as it is possible to talk about the impact of such parties on the political arena, it is likely that media that exhibit similar traits (anti-establishment rhetoric, a message that undermines confidence in the prevailing order and positions that are very far from the others actors) contribute to increased polarization in the public debate that is conducted via media in a society. We can see that there are major differences in how the different actors relate to the current order and to what extent this is challenged. These are issues that need to be investigated more closely and accurately in future studies. But what do we already know about these things, in relation to right-wing alternative media?

Populism and alternative media

One of the areas that have actually been researched quite extensively during recent years is the relationship between media and populism. Again, Trump serves as the go-to example with his connections to and support from various alternative media outlets, like *Breitbart News Network*, but also *Infowars*, where he appeared for an interview during the campaign. Most research studies, however, tend to focus on the relationship between the mass media mainstream and populist politicians, and how media plays an important part in laying the ground for populist rhetoric to be successful (see Aalberg et al., 2016; Krämer, 2017, 2018). There is less research on the link between populism and alternative media, though the link is quite clear in some cases. Populism is a concept that can take on many meanings. Knigge (1998) observes that the term populism applied to right-wing movements tends to be overlapping other labels, such as "right-wing radicalism," "right-wing extremism" and even "neo-fascism" (Knigge, 1998, p. 250). There is a debate about whether or not these terms are adequate synonyms, especially when applied to certain political parties who appear as "extreme rightist" within a given party system, but would themselves object strongly to such labels. Taguieff (1998) talks about populism as "the appeal to the people, at the same time as demos and as ethnos, against the elites, and against the foreigners" (p. 5).[1] Mudde defines populism as a "thin ideology" that "considers society to be ultimately separated into two homogeneous and antagonistic groups, 'the pure people' versus 'the corrupt elite', and which argues that politics should be an expression of the volonté générale (general will) of the people" (Mudde, 2004, p. 543). Pivotal for the possibility of this dichotomization is the notion of the "Heartland," the interpretation of "the people" as a group of genuine, sensible, honest and hardworking ordinary people, who have become reduced to passive onlookers of a process of gradual deterioration of a stable system, caused by societal elites who, in various ways, represent "special interests" (Mudde, 2004). In his description of the causes for the success of populist politicians in western liberal democracies, he highlights Cappella and Jamieson's (1996) notion of a spiral of cynicism, caused by the role played by media in society: "more important than the actual increase in sleaze and corruption in politics" (p. 553), Mudde argues, is the fact that media tends to report on politics in a sensationalist way, with a focus on negative news and scandals. Media companies had gone from transmitting news from the elites to the people, to an increase in content that ultimately feeds populist sentiments, and skepticism towards the political elite (See also Krämer, 2014). Since 2004, the role of traditional media has faced a dramatic process of redefinition caused by the rise of social media, where content produced by "grassroots" and distributed through online social networks has gained importance and challenged traditional media.

Research points to an important relationship between right-wing populists and right-wing media, especially in the online sphere is emerging (Krämer, 2017; Mazzoleni, 2014). Right-wing alternative media is becoming more and more professionalized when it comes to organization and PR. In American politics for example, representative alternative right-wing media outlets have gained access to the White House on the policy level (former *Breitbart* leader, Steve Bannon was for a while very close to the Trump administration) (Haller & Holt, 2018). Here, it is clear that populist politicians players strategically seek relationships to these media: Alternative media serves to bypass the logic of the mainstream media. It can also signal distance from "the elite" to supporters who are critical of the mainstream, a view that is clearly related to the populist attitude (Jagers & Walgrave, 2007).

Reach and impact

One of the best sources we have for information about the reach of alternative media is the Reuters Institute for the Study of Journalism's yearly Digital News Report (Newman, Fletcher, Kalogeropoulos, Levy, & Kleis Nielsen, 2018). In the 2018 version, a special focus on "alternative" and "partisan" brands was introduced and the report includes data from a range of countries about the reach (as measured by use during the last week) and brand trust for alternative media brands in comparison with more traditional mainstream/legacy media brands. One of the first things to strike the reader is that alternative media is very often right-wing leaning, although there are examples of left-leaning alternative media as well. The situation also varies depending on what country is studied. In Spain for example, traditional mainstream media has been in decline for a long period of time, and therefore, a wide range of alternative partisan media with a focus on news and views have seen the light during a longer period of time and also of a wider diversity than compared to, for example, the alternative media studied in Sweden in the same report (Newman et al., 2018).

What does the data tell us? In the US, the two most famous right-wing alternative media brands, *Breitbart News Network* and *Infowars*, do not seem to be particularly widespread in terms of usership. *Breitbart News Network* was started in 2007 and is known for its support for Donald Trump, a number of controversial stories that have been shown to be false and have become sort of an emblem of right-wing alternative media and stock example of how such media can be successful in shaping opinions. It primarily targets the mainstream media, the Democratic Party and the Republican establishment in Washington (seen as part of "the swamp"). And their reporting focuses especially on Hollywood, the government, "big journalism" and national security from a right-wing and strongly conservative viewpoint.[2] *Infowars* is a website run by Alex Jones, who is believer in the conspiracy theory about a New World Order, espoused by certain fractions of the fringe right. Having started as a radio-show host in the 1990s, *Infowars* was launched in 1999 and Jones is still the publisher and director of the site, while employing others, such as YouTube personality Paul Joseph Watson as editors and contributing writers. The site has been reported to have millions of unique visitors monthly (Beauchamp, 2016). In the Reuter's study, 7% of the respondents from the US reported using *Breitbart News Network* to access news in the last week. Three per cent said the same about *Infowars*. On the other hand, 45% reported having heard of *Breitbart* and 29% had heard about *Infowars* (Newman et al., 2018, p. 20). At least looking at these right-wing alternative media from a national perspective, *Breitbart News Network* and *Infowars* seem to be substantially more famous than they are actually being used.

In the UK, the situation is a bit different. The most important right-wing alternative media, *Breitbart UK* and *Westmonster*, have competition from left-leaning alternative media such as *The Canary, Another Angry Voice* and *Evolve Politics* and were actively both used by 2% of the population. Again, the number of people in the UK who reported having heard of *Breitbart* (19%) is much larger than the usage, while the site *Westmonster* only was known by 6% of the population. In Germany, Breitbart Germany was known by 17% of the population but only used actively for news by 1%. The German sites *Junge Freiheit* (used by 3%), *Politically Incorrect* ("PI-News", used by 2%) and *Compact online* (also used by 2%) actually have a higher usage by Germans although Breitbart is far more widely known. In all of these countries, right-wing alternative media come across as having a clearly marginal readership on a national level. A country that stands out a bit from the other studied countries is Sweden where the most important alternative right-wing media reach up to 12% of the population (*Fria Tider*, the biggest with 12%, *Nyheter Idag* around 10%).

Another way of measuring impact in comparison with mainstream media is to look at social media interactions. Here there have been several studies from various countries that show that users of social media, especially Twitter and Facebook, like, share and comment on content from alternative media sources to a degree that is in some cases comparable to some of the most important mainstream media outlets (sources). Such studies, however, must be treated with some coolness, since they only measure the activities on social media, and not the whole population and therefore cannot be taken as indication of the total impact in society. *Breitbart News,* for example, famously boasted interactivity numbers that outdid major brands such as Fox News, *The New York Times* and *Washington Post* on the election night 2016 – they were number four on the list of "Biggest Election Day Publishers" on Facebook, only outperformed by NBC, The Huffington Post and *USA Today* (Nash, 2016). Studies have compared how mainstream and alternative news are shared on social media (Zannettou et al., 2017, 2018). Through analysis of several millions of posts alternative and mainstream news interactions were measured on Twitter, Reddit and 4chan. The results show that especially groups of users on 4chan and Reddit had a high level of impact news that were shared on Twitter, mostly linking to alternative news. Such dynamics can help explain the success of alternative media in terms of interactivity measures on social media – they have groups of active users who also push for the content to spread it to others.

The audience

Reuters Institute for the study of Journalism's report looks at further data and also presents some interesting findings about the audience. The audiences of right-wing alternative media in all studied countries have political and ideological worldviews that are clearly more to the right compared to the audience of the most wide-reaching mainstream media. It clearly seems that right-wing alternative media cater to specific audiences. German scholar Haller (2017) made the claim that right-wing alternative media in Germany existed because there was a demand for news and views with a perspective that corresponded to groups of readers that the mainstream media failed to address in a way that was resonated with what they thought was important (Haller, 2017). This is consistent with findings presented by Jennifer Rauch (2015), one of the few scholars who have looked into how the audience construes notions about alternative and mainstream media. Her findings point out two important things: First, the "dialectic of alternative media/mainstream media continues to provide a critical and cultural touchstone for users in a converged environment," and second, respondents valued alternative content ("neglected issues, diverse voices, mobilizing information") highly. What the users mean by "alternative media" differs though, as some considered, even news outlets like Fox News as "alternative media." The most important attributes of alternative media, according to the Rauch's respondents, were that they were "Devoted to issues and events not discussed elsewhere" and that they "Allow a wide range of people to express their voices and opinions" (Rauch, 2015, p. 133).

The audience of right-wing alternative media is quite under-researched, and there are not many studies available that can give us more information about their media use – questions like if they only turn to alternative media or if they merely include them in their news diet in order to compare perspectives need to be looked into more thoroughly in order to gain better understanding. One study looked specifically at how Christian conservatives in the US used Google as a resource for fact-checking the news from mainstream media, and in that pursuit, alternative media, like YouTube videos from *PragerU* who particularly creates content with this specific audience in mind, provided them with points of comparisons and other perspectives (Tripodi, 2018).[3]

Extremist right-wing alternative media

As stated in the previous chapter, this type of media is both extreme and influential at the same time, having an anti-system agenda as well as an anti-system impact and effect on the surrounding media landscape – a combination that is quite rare. While there has been some research done on extreme right-wing media, most of them focus on fringe groups and their media outlets and it is difficult to find studies on alternative media that match both of these criteria. Nordfront.se is the official homepage of the Swedish organization Nordiska Motståndsrörelsen (NMR – the Nordic Resistance Movement), an organization with clear and outspoken adherence to Nazism, or "national socialism" as they prefer to call it (Nordfront.se). The organization has branches in Finland (although it was outlawed in 2017), Norway, Denmark and Iceland and also operates an English-speaking version aimed at an international audience. In Sweden the organization is also a political party. NMR is a very small group; in the general election in 2018, they received 2,106 votes in total and the number of members in the organization itself is estimated to around 159, and the movement seems to have attracted new recruits recently (Arias, Åkerman, & Karlsson, 2016). Their ideology is clearly anti-system, both in terms of the political project (they want to overturn society through revolution) and in their vision about a completely new media system (for example, they want to "cleanse" the journalistic profession from traitors, expropriate the property of media organizations deemed as hostile to the people, make it illegal for foreigners to own media, prosecute journalists that are deemed to have participated in hostile propaganda, etc.). In September 2018, a member of the NMR, who carefully mapped two journalists, was sentenced for gross crime. Clearly, this is a marginal group on the outer fringe of the ideological spectrum (Mattsson, 2018).

The homepage Nordfront.se has been active since 1997 (although previously under another name) and serves as the major outlet for propaganda and information for members. Typically, it reports on current events about issues of relevance for the organization (immigration, Zionism, homosexuality). The articles frequently comment on news published in the mainstream media in a reactive fashion often with the intent of correcting descriptions that are perceived as false or publish rewrites from other media, especially *Russia Today* is frequently referred to in the articles. They also do radio broadcasts and pods available through the homepage and run a YouTube channel N TV that has 605 followers.

In my view, the most interesting thing about Nordfront.se is not their extreme views or their inflammatory language. This is pretty much what is to be expected from the media outlet of outspoken organized Nazis. It is rather the attention they manage to attract from other people than the few activists that are actually a part of the NMR that is relevant. In relation to the size of this organization (comparable in numbers to any other small club for people with very peculiar common interests), the NMR has managed to do many things that have attracted the interest or outrage from large groups of people in society and as a result much media coverage. In 2018 alone, the media outlet Nordfront.se was mentioned in 1,085 Swedish news articles (mainstream printed press, web, radio and TV sources), according to a search in the media archive Retriever. Over the last three years, the number of articles about Nordfront.se is over 4,000. Note that this is simply about the media outlet Nordfront.se itself, the number of articles about the organization NMR is over 33,000. A substantial amount of these articles are related to covering some of the spectacular marches and other public appearances of some of the members of the NMR or controversies and debates that have arisen as a consequence of them. The most striking example of this is when hundreds of NMR members and supporters marched in Gothenburg at the same time as the ongoing Gothenburg Book Fair in September 2017 (the reported number of participants in march varies from around 200 to 650, depending on the source) – only weeks after the tumultuous Unite the Right rally in Charlottesville, Virginia, that had caused headlines around the world. The originally planned route for the NMR march included passing by the Synagogue in Gothenburg, and after much debate and protest from various debaters and actors, the police decided to only allow a shorter and less controversial route for the demonstration on September 30. Since there had already been so much debate, a lot of protesters were expected to show up (reported numbers range from 15,000 to 20,000 protesters).

Naturally, the whole context and timing of the march and the controversial nature of the group made the event highly newsworthy, and the coverage was massive in all the mainstream media channels. The march did not last long, after a short time the demonstrators tried to break off from the prescribed route and were stopped and transported away in buses. Police officers and activists were injured, and a number were arrested, leading to a legal after play, also covered widely in the media.

This was how the Nordfront.se editorial triumphantly summarized the event afterwards as a "success" in an anonymous editorial:

> Already before the day itself, the mainstream media's hysteria had made the name 'Nordic Resistance Movement' known to the whole population. During the day, Nordfront TV's livestream trended and was the second most watched clip on YouTube in the world.[4]

> (Nordfront.se, 2017)

Needless to point out, this event was of course part of a communication plan, like other NMR events that have also resulted in a high degree of attention from other media. By deliberately choosing a provocative time and place for the march (during the Gothenburg Book Fair, one of the largest in northern Europe and consequently a major event where a lot of the media's focus is already on what is happening there) and a controversial original route (passing by a synagogue) they managed to build up an anticipation of the event in advance. The Charlottesville riots of course, incidentally, contributed to making the event extra intersecting for a large audience at that time. During the march itself, the activists wore plastic shields with the Nordfront.se web address printed so that the cameras could not miss it.

Using the terminology from Chapter 3, Nordfront.se is by all standards a case of an obviously marginal phenomena – it is the media outlet of a fringe group with an extreme and subversive ideology, making it the perfect example of what I call "irrelevant alternative media." But given the amount of attention they have managed to attract; the classification becomes tricky.

The "alt-right," "new right" and "metapolitics"

Although far-right extremism online is often easy to spot, and the violent propaganda it contains is easy to detect, the way the groups and organizations behind these kinds of websites behave, especially those who have branched into social media, is not always easily categorized as hate speech and violent. As other researchers have pointed out, the social media of white supremacists and other like-minded groups constitute social networks of people who not only concentrate on ideology but also share recipes, poems and movie reviews, much like in other online social forums – creating a sense of community. Meddaugh and Kay (2009) showed in their analysis of the (now defunct) white nationalist online community Stormfront.org that discourse on Stormfront "appears less virulent and more palatable to the naive reader," and that it:

> provides a 'cyber transition' between traditional hate speech and 'reasonable racism,' a tempered discourse that emphasizes pseudo rational discussions of race, and subsequently may cast a wider net in attracting audiences.
>
> (p. 251)

Some actors in the field of right-wing alternative media, especially those leaning towards an identitarian worldview, have actively adopted Gramscian analysis of hegemony and turned it into an operative strategy called metapolitics (Griffin, 2000; Holt, 2017). This notion is particularly interesting in relation to the topic at hand, and in light of the previous description of the very clearly Gramscian underpinnings of much research about alternative media. The French *Nouvelle Droite* movement's front – figure, Alain de Benoist[5] – identified the need to mobilize a "new right" in the light of the fact that universities as well as the media and politics were generally dominated so totally by the left that in principle it was impossible to do successful opinion formation at all with conventional methods (Griffin, 2000). De Benoist explicitly argued that a new strategy was needed – then turned to Gramsci. The idea was to study how the left had worked to get the dominant position they had managed to get and then imitate it. He called the strategy for "metapolitics."[6]

Since many of the positions that he himself represented (e.g. ethnically homogenous communities should grow isolated from each other and not be mixed) could easily be defined as illegitimate, the first step was to break the hegemony that locked him into rhetorically problematic positions already in advance defined as fascist. This is not done in an instant, but the culture needs to be processed over a long period of time to successfully build an acceptance for alternative concepts and reality depictions. "Ethnopluralism" is an example of such a word: In order not to be accused of being racist or fascist, the Benoist strongly argues against racism and points out that human value can never be linked to external attributes such as skin tone. He points out, however, that there are many different ethnic groups with a distinctive character – and that the American "melting pot" ideal will result in a single large blend that shatters ethnic identities. In order to preserve diversity, according to de Benoist, it is important to protect the European peoples against excessive immigration from other ethnic groups (de Benoist & Champetier, 1999).

Metapedia.org, the alternative identitarian online encyclopedia, is a good example of how such metapolitical action can take shape. It has borrowed its collaborative and participatory structure, from Wikipedia. But it has a "metapolitical purpose, to influence the mainstream debate, culture and historical view" by providing an alternative description of the world (Metapedia). It has been operative since 2006 and offers entries in 20 "European languages," and it states, in a pledge for Bitcoin donations on their front-page, that: "In the Internet Age, the control and distribution of information is vital for political interests, as well as cultural and racial survival. Metapedia is the only major encyclopedia to challenge the mainstream narratives, proliferating across the media landscape" (Metapedia).

As Dahlgren and Alvares (2015) point out groups can espouse values that are not progressive or liberal, "whilst nevertheless remaining 'publics'" (p. 6). In some outspokenly far-right movements Metapolitics is a concept that illustrates this notion. Metapolitics is defined by activists (Bernsand, 2013; Iost, 2012) as an idea of a cultural battle, a communicative strategy to counter a perceived marginalization by hegemonic discourse (Bernsand, 2013; Griffin, 2000). It is a concept that is adopted from the French "nouvelle droite" (especially Alain de Benoist) and refers to the waging of a long-term cultural battle rather than a purely political one. Related to metapolitics is the notion of identitarianism, defined in the English section of Metapedia.org as:

> a term used to refer to a European New Right movement and its sympathizers. It holds the preservation and development of ethnic and cultural identity as its central ideological principle, and criticizes the state of the contemporary West.
>
> (Metapedia.org)

Metapolitics is a communicative strategy, developed to counter a perceived marginalization by hegemonic media discourse (Bernsand, 2013; Griffin, 2000). According to Metapedia, "Activities such as creating culture and influencing public opinion in fields not normally considered part of the political sphere have therefore become an essential part of the identitarian project" (Metapedia.org). Metapolitics is a cultural struggle, designed to influence culture and discourse in a longer time frame (Griffin, 2000). The aim is to prepare society for future political intervention by slowly building up a cultural acceptance for alternative descriptions of reality. In this struggle, mainstream media is the singular most important adversary.

In many of the articles found in this "alternative encyclopedia," mainstream media narratives are taken apart and criticized as misleading and orchestrated by elites in order to achieve consensus. One example is the notion of the "The demographic bomb" which, according to Metapedia, is presented as a concept used to justify mass immigration in order to secure a labour force for the future. Counterarguments are presented, and the article argues that such expressions functions as a front for the agenda of "people exchange politics," where the ultimate goal is to slowly replace the indigenous white population in European countries with foreign people. Metapolitics is not new – it is cultural propaganda, but through social media the possibilities of reaching out are historically new and can be related to Downey and Fenton's (2003) definition of "counter-public spheres":

> Once the public sphere is defined as a horizon for the organization of social experience, it follows that there are multiple and competing counter publics, each marked by specific terms of exclusion (for example, those of class, race, gender) in relation to dominant communications, yet each understanding itself as a nucleus for an alternative organization of society.
>
> (Downey & Fenton, 2003, p. 194)

Alternative and participatory media is an important channel for metapolitics and a manifestation of the metapolitical project as part of the formation of right-wing counter-public spheres. While metapolitics is an important notion regarding the far-right end of the spectrum, such as identitarian movements, these movements need to be distinguished from others, such as right-wing populists who pursue their aims within the sphere of democratic politics. The core of the metapolitical struggle, as visible in the case of Metapedia.org, is to offer new space for "participation" that lies beyond the borders of mainstream opinion formation, and thus also outside the sphere of democratic political participation and civic engagement – metapolitical participation is therefore in a sense oxymoronic. It calls for participation outside the realm of the political, which is the origin of the notion of participation as an ideal (Mouffe, 2013). On the other hand, the metapolitical struggle is construed, by identitarians, as a survival strategy for a period of "interregnum" that will last until a future arrives that will dawn after the debauchery, corruption and general decay of modern democracies inevitably has led to chaos (Griffin, 2000).

In the Christchurch shooter's manifesto, there are several references to identitarianism and a metapolitical approach to changing society. It must be understood as a long-term struggle, of slowly altering culture and by introducing and disseminating new definitions of themselves and others, thus paving the way for future political activity. So, metapolitics is in no way apolitical either, since it presupposes a future triumph. It could be called über-politics, in a hubristic Nietzschean sense. Metapolitical participation in cases such as Metapedia must therefore be included in the registry of manifestations of the changing ways in which alternative participatory online media involve citizens. This approach – by using new words and approaches, and thus creating new communicative options for ideas that are generally classified as beyond what is commonly accepted – is currently well-known and discussed (see, for example, Griffin, 2000) but worth mentioning in today's discussion about media criticism and distrust. Much of what the alt-right does can be called metapolitics, especially the use of memes and trolling as a way of breaking taboos in order to push the borders of acceptability (Nagle, 2018).

Propaganda and disinformation

As we noted earlier, in much previous theory, the notion of "propaganda" would probably mostly be associated with the mainstream media, rather than alternative media. Herman and Chomsky's propaganda model, for example, clearly points out the mainstream media as a system for propaganda. However, in today's debate, there has been a clear shift, even within academic discourse. Alternative media is more often pointed out as a potential threat precisely because it can be a powerful tool for propaganda, and vice versa; the mainstream media is more often described in research and political and journalistic discourse as a bulwark of truth in the face of fake news and disinformation. As the American investigations into Russian attempts to interfere in their election campaign 2016 illustrates, foreign powers can of course use alternative media to disseminate messages aimed at creating turmoil, confusion and chaos in another country (Faris et al., 2017). In this context, cases like *Russia Today (RT)* and *Sputnik News* are highly interesting because they exemplify that some alternative media might be directly run by foreign powers, while others might be quite influenced by their more official outlets (such as RT), as sources of news. Studies that have tried to measure attempts at propaganda during the Swedish election in 2018, for example, point out that there were limited attempts to influence Swedish voters, although much of the automated traffic (bots) tended to support the indigenous immigration critical alternative media, rather than promoting content of Russian origin (Colliver, Pomerantsev, Applebaum, & Birdwell, 2018). An issue that has been discussed much since the US presidential election in 2016 is how social media can act as channels for disinformation and especially for important elections acting as propaganda channels (especially for Russian interests). In combination with today's opportunities to tailor campaign material to specific target groups on social media ("microtargeting," see Fulgoni, Lipsman, & Davidsen, 2016), based on advanced analysis of data that people themselves submit to companies such as Google and Facebook, the possibilities appear to the influence of alien power as alarming. In the analyzes of influencing operations prior to the US election in 2016, a number of more or less successful attempts to influence American public opinion could be identified. These mainly aimed at spreading confusion and fuelled the polarization between the political blocks (Faris et al., 2017).

The studies that have so far tried to look at it show that there are some, but limited, attempts by the Russian side to spread propaganda in different networks (Fernquist, Kaati, Akrami, Cohen, & Schroeder, 2018). As in the US, robot traffic is shared, sharing information from known Russian channels, but only to a very limited extent. Automated robot traffic ("bots") on Twitter accounted for about 11% of all traffic, and they shared more information from the domestic immigration critical alternative media than ordinary users do. A report that studied sharing on Twitter prior to the Swedish election in 2018 also shows that Swedish non-robot accounts also share more news from domestic alternative media than any other European country (Hedman, Sivnert & Howard, 2018). A little more than one-fifth (22%) of all posts during important hashtags prior to the election included links to various immigrant critical alternative media. Of these, 87% could be derived from one of the three largest: *Fria Tider, Nyheter Idag* or *Samhällsnytt*. The picture is thus complex.

It is clear that bots are used in social media to spread certain perspectives for the purpose of influence, while studies have shown that the effect of these did not play any crucial role for the election results. An American study shows that those who take part in such content via social media (on average one to a few articles per US citizen during the months of the 2016 election) assess the content primarily based on already established interpretation patterns predisposed by already existing political sympathies (Allcott & Gentzkow, 2017). Approximately one in four Americans once visited a site containing disinformation, but the figure is a little misleading because it was mainly a small group of people (10%) who accounted for the lion's share of these visits, while the vast majority never had contact with this type of material.

As a challenge for journalism, this phenomenon is thus partly linked to the emergence of the alternative media discussed above, since the studies that have been done so far point to the fact that it is not primarily Russian propaganda sources, but rather domestic alternative media that benefit from the admittedly modest, yet clear influence operations that have been identified. Rather, the challenge here is not so much about a threat to established journalism as a problem with finding an approach that helps more than it harms. There are several problems involved in this balance act – which have to do with the very starting point of the debate, namely concepts such as "fake news" and "junk news" (Lazer et al., 2018).

Fake news is fake because of its fakeness...

"Fake news" has become such an infected concept that many believe that it cannot be used anymore, because it is not possible to agree on what is meant by the term. Is it, as Trump and many alternative media claim, the mainstream media's left-wing, politically correct and didactic form of news reporting? Or is it, as many politicians and journalists mean, rather the rightist forces' alarmist descriptions of society's imminent disintegration due to the high immigration to Sweden/Europe/West? The term is mostly used as a baseball bat to undermine the opponent's descriptions of reality. The problem is that such a starting point (regardless of which camp does it) is based on a circular way of reasoning: The allegedly fake is considered fake because of its alleged fakeness. What is needed is rather a constructive way to move on from just stating that there are reality descriptions that do not correspond to reality and that it is a problem that this occurs (among others).

The expression "fake news" was in fact not much used until quite recently. Journalist Sharyl Attkisson (2017) claims that it was not until October 2016 that it first started becoming a highly used search term on Google (an observation that is undeniable when studying the interest over time for "fake news" on Google trends). Attkisson, quite convincingly, explains the sudden interest for this particular phrase as the result of a successful PR effort to put this concept on the public agenda for political reasons, and with the intent of smearing especially conservative media outlets. In any case, false news reporting has of course always occurred since the dawn of journalism (and arguably long before that). It has caused great damage throughout the ages – from the smearing of religious opponents during the European 30-year war of the 17th century to modern scandal-focused sensational journalism selling on spreading unconfirmed rumors of known (and sometimes unknown) people. False news has always existed within the framework of established media as well as part of propaganda operations and can take many different forms. In Sweden, for example, the tabloid *Aftonbladet*'s glorifying descriptions of Nazi Germany during the 1930s and the leading morning paper *Dagens Nyheter*'s blatantly uncritical and celebratory reports from the Cultural Revolution in Communist China in the 1970s are examples of news reporting with a most suspicious attitude towards truth as well as totalitarian foreign powers. To attach the label of fake news only to alternative media is therefore simplistic and one-sided.

Thinking critically about news in order to counter false information, therefore, cannot be reduced to the making of lists of news providers that someone thinks are credible versus not credible – this is to make things way too comfortable. Relying on self-proclaimed factual investigators who in various ways reveal fake news is not enough either. Efforts such as Snopes, NewsGuard, firstdraftnews.org or the now defunct Swedish faktiskt.se (which is based on the Norwegian faktisk.no and which was run by several large media companies in collaboration) can indeed serve as a reference point for the interested citizen who already relies heavily on the large media companies to a large extent. But one has to remember that for others, the project runs the risk of appearing as another way of trying to control public discourse by defining "wrong" views as "false," especially if these operations are run by organizations and people associated with elite mainstream politicians and journalists. In order for such efforts to be meaningful, they must not only be, but also be regarded as trustworthy and impartial (Lazer et al., 2018). Neither of these conditions are self-evidently true to a large number of people.

Indeed, there is a strong perception by many, especially conservative or otherwise right-wing media that this is exactly what is going on. The recent movie *Hoaxed* (2019) is a good example, in which controversial citizen reporter and alternative media figure Mike Cernovich (who was involved in the dissemination of the infamous Pizzagate story) interviews a number of actors that have been labelled as fake news creators and manipulators, creating a counter-narrative to the one most commonly upheld in mainstream media. This points to one of the problems that it will be very difficult to reach any form of consensus about how to define fake news that manage to bridge ideological and political division. Shin and Thorson (2017), in a study, show that people who share articles on Twitter from various fact-checkers and often are openly critical of the organizations that do the fact-checking and also systematically select the articles that show that their political opponents have said something wrong, and avoid sharing articles about their own party so-called "selective sharing" (Shin & Thorson, 2017). Another problem is that these have a hard time attracting the attention of the audience in the information noise that surrounds them, so even if they are there and actually do a good job, they might not get noticed (Vargo, Guo, & Amazeen, 2017).

The interest for fake news in research is also interesting to study from a historical perspective. A Google scholar search for the exact phrase "fake news" returns 16,500 results dated 1945 or later. The same search with the interval 2016–2019 returns 10,980 results. When comparing articles from before 2016 and after, it is striking how the focus seems to have changed. Some pre-2016 articles already addressed the notion of fake news as disinformation by malevolent actors (Lazer et al., 2018), but more typically it addressed issues like VNR's and fake news as satire. These figures are not a definite measure and must be treated with some care, but they certainly do suggest a strong correlation in time between public interest in the phenomenon and a jump in research interest about this topic, and that the interest has also grown dramatically for different ways of actively working against it.

Another term that has been used recently in research is "junk news," and although not as widely used, its usage also has an interesting development over time. While Natalie Fenton used the word in a book title from 2009, about the overall poor quality of much mainstream media news, it has taken on a more specific meaning in relation to "computational propaganda" since 2016, at least when looking at how it is used in scholarly work. Howard and Bradshaw (2017) talk about computational propaganda that distributes "large amounts of misinformation about politics and public policy over social media platforms" (p. 1). They point out that the combination of automation and propaganda can significantly impact public opinion. Their definition of junk news that has been used to code shared twitter content during a number of election campaigns goes like this:

> Junk News. This content includes various forms of propaganda and ideologically extreme, hyper-partisan, or conspiratorial political news and information. Much of this content is deliberately

produced false reporting. It seeks to persuade readers about the moral virtues or failings of organizations, causes or people and presents commentary as a news product. This content is produced by organizations that do not employ professional journalists, and the content uses attention grabbing techniques, lots of pictures, moving images, excessive capitalization, ad hominem attacks, emotionally charged words and pictures, unsafe generalizations and other logical fallacies.

(p. 3)

According to this particular study, the French shared less "junk news" during the election campaign in 2017 compared to the Americans in 2016. However, this kind of characterization is highly problematic, since all of these characteristics, except for not employing "professional journalists", could indeed be used about mainstream news outlets as well as alternative media. The study is a part of a larger project called the "Computational Propaganda Project" at the Oxford Internet Institute, and this is just one of many similar analyses (other examined countries are, among others, Sweden, Mexico, the US, the UK and Germany). From their research design descriptions, it becomes clear that the way they code the shared Twitter content during the selected periods is based on a judgement of the source rather than content – in other words, established news media seem to be automatically excluded, since the junk news is only used as a category for coding other sources than established news media. Such a division will probably not appear as especially convincing to many of the alternative media producers or their frequent readers.

Filter bubbles and echo chambers

"Alternative" is an epithet that should be interpreted as a signal of a relationship of opposition against the "establishment" rather than laying claim to substitution and equivalence. The existence of the "alternative" and its position thus presupposes the existence and position of "the Original" (mainstream) in order to be meaningful. But even if the worldview presented is different in that it focuses on some specific aspects, it is not completely different or cut off from MSM either. Interesting to note in this context is that several studies have shown that alternative media very often contain references to and build on articles from more established journalistic media – it indicates that they largely also depend on the "old media" in order to have something to write about. The relationship of opposition against the established media is thus also, necessarily, a relationship of dependence (Haller & Holt, 2018; Holt, 2017). Also, these references to mainstream media are not primarily of a hostile nature, but often neutral in tone – although selected because they deal with specific issue (immigration, for example). This suggests that, in addition to criticizing the "mainstream," they simply use the material published there for their own use, much like the general trend in web journalism, where more and more material is in fact recycled rewrites of stories and news produced by others (Karlsson & Holt, 2016). Alternative media are therefore undoubtedly part of a wider media ecology, where the agenda still originates to a large extent from the big established journalistic mainstream media, and where alternative media mostly react to stories, topics and views expressed by others rather than setting the agenda themselves. In relation to concerns about balkanization (Sunstein, 2007), echo chambers (Jamieson & Cappella, 2008) and filter bubbles (Pariser, 2011) this is an interesting observation. Although alternative media might be very good examples of echo chambers, it is clear that what is echoed often originates from mainstream media to a high degree (Haller & Holt, 2018; Holt, 2016a; von Nordheim, Müller, & Scheppe, 2019). Although these media potentially epitomize what is meant by cyberbalkanization (closed off places where people with similar views entrench themselves in digital bubbles, and therefore avoid contact with those who disagree), the empirical evidence suggests that they are not insular, but that the borders between spheres are indeed porous.

The Intellectual Dark Web

As implied in previous chapters, not all alternative media that are attributed right-wing sympathies are extreme and malicious, like the cases described above. The participant of the network called the Intellectual Dark Web is a good example of this. Debaters who are often listed as members of this network are as diverse characters as Jordan Peterson, Dave Rubin, Sam Harris, Ben Shapiro, Douglas Murray and number of others. These characters differ on a number of questions, such as their views on religion (some are outspoken atheists, while some are vocal about their beliefs), morality (the abortion issue, for example), as well as where they stand ideologically in relation to conservatism and libertarianism. What they have in common, according to their own descriptions (and the famous article by Weiss in NYT), is that they see themselves as "renegades" who have been ousted from mainstream platforms as a consequence of stating uncomfortable facts and

opinions. Mathematician Eric Weinstein, who is attributed with nam-
ing the network, describes the general observation in an interview with
David Fuller, who runs the YouTube channel *Rebel Wisdom*:

> … so, we have gotten to a completely crazy stage whereby people
> who hold absolutely garden variety, common sense viewpoints,
> are seeing themselves reflected in the media as if in a funhouse
> mirror. And they are seeing themselves come back so distorted
> and ugly that they are asking, "What just happened, I fell asleep
> for a few years and I wake up Rip van Winkle style, and I am in a
> world in which I am suddenly the bad guy for simply holding very
> commonplace ideas."
>
> (Fuller, 2018)

The idea of the Intellectual Dark Web is built around the notion
of free speech and the free exchange of ideas, even those that are
considered too controversial in many media outlets. They primarily
meet each other, and other people who hold controversial beliefs that
they themselves do not necessarily agree with, in the spirit of test-
ing arguments against each other, while remaining civil even in case
of disagreement. *The Rubin Report*, a YouTube channel with currently around 974,000 subscribers, hosted by comedian Dave Rubin
is something of a meeting place for many of such discussions. The
show is described as "… the largest talk show about free speech and
big ideas on YouTube" (*The Rubin Report*, YouTube). The show has
interviewed a host of controversial figures such as Stefan Molyneux
(a Canadian YouTube personality with a focus on philosophy and
questions related to race and IQ) and UK-based Tommy Robinson,
the founder of the English Defence League (which he is no longer
a member of), as well as more established figures such as Tucker
Carlson and Stephen Pinker. Rebecca Lewis (2018) argues that the
members of the Intellectual Dark Web are part of a larger "Alternative Influence Network" (AIN):

> This network is connected through a dense system of guest ap-
> pearances, mixing content from a variety of ideologies. This
> cross-promotion of ideas forms a broader "reactionary" position: a
> general opposition to feminism, social justice, or left-wing politics.
>
> (Lewis, 2018, p. 1)

According to Lewis, the AIN serves as a larger net, where the audience can be drawn in and through watching interactions between

less radical figures and more radical ones in a chummy and polite way – a strategy employed to make extreme ideas seems less dangerous, but rather "framed as lighthearted, entertaining, rebellious, and fun" (p. 1). This is, however, not necessarily the case. One of the most viewed episodes of *The Rubin Report*, for example, is when Dave Rubin (who is homosexual and married to a man) has a "sit down" with conservative Jewish debater Ben Shapiro on the topic of gay marriage. Obviously the two did not agree on the issue, but both explained their positions at length in a discussion that clearly laid out the rationales for both positions for the viewers. In fact, this is the typical approach of various sit downs between members of the Intellectual Dark Web and other, more controversial figures. The proposition that interactions by these YouTube celebrities, with self-advertised white nationalists or supremacists, for example, imply a secret tactic to normalize extremist positions is not only contrary to what the members of the network state themselves in their videos, but it is also based on the premise that interaction with someone implies collaboration and endorsement of their views.

As an example of alternative media producers that are counted as right-wing (although, not all members of the Intellectual Dark Web identify as right-wing), I would rather classify them as simply alternative media, and not as having anti-system or polarizing characteristics. The ideological convergence of these figures tends to revolve around the value of free speech and academic freedom – often in response to left-wing activism on campuses, issues of censorship and political correctness gone too far. The issues they raise, however, touch upon the topic of the next chapter: How do "the elites" that so many of the right-wing alternative media criticize react to their existence.

Notes

1 "l'appel au peuple, à la fois comme démos et comme ethnos, contre les élites et contre les étrangers" (p. 5).
2 The classification of *Breitbart* has been done in many ways, it has been called populist, alt-right, Ultra-conservative, white supremacist by some, while they themselves refute such labels.
3 Prager University is not a university, but a conservative organization, started by radio host Dennis Prager as an attempt to counter the effects of leftist dominance on universities. The channel has, as of March 2019, 657,360,219 views of its videos. *PragerU* is one example of a conservative YouTube channel that had videos removed on unclear grounds, leading to controversy. The videos were later made available again.
4 The video itself seems to be unavailable, so I have not been able to verify the claim.

5 Alain de Benoist has been written about issues related to ethnicity, European culture and politics. He was one of the leaders in the GRECE (Groupement de recherche et d'études pour la civilisation européenne) – an association founded in 1968. He has figured in many contexts, including as a writer in le Figaro. His thinking has had a lot of influence in many movements, usually placed to the right of the "mainstream right." Concepts such as ethnopluralism, metapolitics and "new right" are directly linked to his thought.

6 The Benoist does not call it a "strategy" himself, but is opposed to such an interpretation, for example, in the Manifesto of the French New Right in Year 2000, he writes:

> Metapolitics is not politics by other means. It is neither a strategy to impose intellectual hegemony, nor an attempt to discredit other possible attitudes or agendas. It rests solely on the premise that ideas play a fundamental role in collective consciousness and, more generally, in human history.
>
> (de Benoist & Champetier, 1999)

On the other hand, the concept is used just as a strategy by many followers. For example, the Swedish Identitarian Wikipedia-like online dictionary Metapedia (as seen in the name) is a direct application of the idea of the metapolitical. To stipulate new concepts and redefine old is the stated purpose of this alternative encyclopedia.

4   Reactions from the mainstream...

The notion of "relational" anti-systemness (see Chapter 2) implies that alternative media can affect the surrounding media landscape simply by existing and causing various reactions from other actors. The impact on public discourse is in many ways determined by how other media position themselves in relation to the particular case of alternative media. If there are no reactions at all, the relational anti-systemness is not of significance and the alternative media might be treated as quite irrelevant. If, on the other hand, they manage to cause a stir, by, for example, attracting harsh criticism and expressions of indignation from mainstream journalists, then their relational anti-systemness is significant and affects public discourse in a polarizing way. But first, we need to contextualize this issue somewhat historically.

All in all, the emergence and apparent success of some right-wing alternative media indicate that we live in a time of great societal change, where much is put on its head. At the same time, they are also an expression of a dynamic that media always had to deal with in different ways – the one that comes from standing in the center of things, telling others about important events in the present and thus having the power to set the agenda for the content of the public conversation and focus.

When the first journalistic companies were established, they built a lucrative business concept. There was a deficit of reliable and up-to-date information (Conboy, 2004). In addition, you could eventually start charging for ads, which created additional revenue. During the golden age of the press and later during the era of broadcast and mass communication, it was a fairly limited number of actors who owned and operated journalist-oriented media companies that created newspapers, and eventually radio and television content. This created both economic conditions for conducting what we today call journalism (critical, independent reporting and examination of everything that is relevant to society as a whole as well as for the individual citizen) and, as a consequence of this, also became a prerequisite for modern democratic national states as we know them today (Carey, 2007). Characteristic of early journalism was that it arose in symbiosis with the emergence of a civic audience, a gathering force that informed about, documented and problematized contemporary events while also interpreting and expressing clear (but also conflicting) positions. Journalism has always been regarded as an opinion barometer, an expression of "public opinion" (Harvard, 2006). Opinions, values and beliefs have therefore always been a part of journalism. As an expression of public opinion, it has also claimed to summarize and express the collective (citizens of a nation state) voice. Therefore, an intense struggle has always been going on between different interests about the privilege of summarizing and expressing the content of this public opinion – a point that has remained at the center of much media criticism. Danish existentialist philosopher Søren Kierkegaard, for example, was highly critical of the press and called notions of "the public" a phantom, in which individuality and difference is lost and levelled and people are reduced to a state of spectatorship (Holt, 2015; Kierkegaard & Hannay, 2001). While there is (in most cases) room for more than one opinion, simplifications are naturally necessary and the room for distinctions is limited. In this discursive warfare over who gets to do the simplifications and generalizations, there have always been winners and losers. Some perspectives/interests/organizations have succeeded better than others, and these have thus gained more influence over designing the starting points for the public conversation and defining what is representative of the larger collective. The losers have simply had to suck it up and regroup for the next battle.

The journalists as actors in the social drama were thus given a special position – on the one hand, as a kind of public self-proclaimed knighthood that protected the interests of the people against potentially tyrannical powers (Lundell, 2002), and, on the other hand, as a Mephistopheles figure, the unpleasant truth-teller who constantly threatens to reveal acts performed in obscurity and who in a sometimes brutal way also exposes the ugly sides of human activity (Peters, 2005). Journalism has therefore always been both loved and supported and at the same time hated and questioned – a double-edged sword which, on the one hand, is an indispensable source of information and understanding (and sometimes even good publicity) but which can also affect each and every one through negative publicity. This has meant that a complex relationship to all forms of authority (political as well as religious or cultural) has constantly forced journalists into a balancing act between different interests – the citizens' information needs, their own survival as well as access to important sources of information (which is often located among the elite) (Carey, 2007). The journalist's room for manoeuver and personal security has often been curtailed in various ways – both through censorship laws and threats of retaliation from various actors that do not appreciate journalistic curiosity and critical perspectives (Ladd, 2010).

On the other hand, it is equally true that journalists of all times and in various ways have misbehaved themselves from time to time – through distorted reporting, the promotion of certain perspectives at the expense of others, lenience towards those in power, failure to examine important societal problems, chasing fame and sensational scoops, which have invited legitimate media criticism and to some extent understandable animosity towards journalists as a collective. Criticism against the media, especially new ones, has been occurring at all times (Holt & von Krogh, 2010), and the price for freedom of the press has always been paid by victims of the excesses committed in its name (Peters, 2005). Criticism is therefore both natural and understandable – what is problematic is when it is used as a reason in order to limit the possibility of free, independent and even unpleasant investigative inquiry through regulations, prohibitions and threats in order to silence uncomfortable views and reality descriptions. The question of how "stoic" it is possible to be in relation to the "abyss" – the different, offensive, threatening and the offensive – has always been central through the history of journalism, but perhaps become more accentuated than ever in today's media landscape (Peters, 2005).

Journalists continue to have a prominent role, but some aspects have changed in the surrounding landscape, which creates new challenges and strains. The business model is not as viable in a situation where it is difficult to get people to pay for the journalistic product. Many of the resources that previously made the journalist role special (access to expensive photo equipment, for example) are not needed in the same way when most mobile phones are equipped with cameras that take high-quality images. Anyone can today do basically the same thing as a journalist and also publish quickly without any major thresholds (Mancini, 2013). Especially when there is dissatisfaction among groups of the population about how professional journalists do their job, this opens up for alternative ways to search for information as well as to publish and spread it. Journalism is therefore exposed to competition in a new way.

Since the arrival of social media, traditional media have faced a dramatic process of redefinition in which content produced by "ordinary people" and distributed through social networks has become increasingly important and challenging traditional media. What trends on social media is also indirectly something that journalistic editors have to relate to – which means a partial shift of power over the agenda – because it is not often material and campaigns that come from sources other than the traditional journalists who succeed in getting impact on social media (Singer, 2013). Professional journalism is increasingly described in terms of decline and crisis (Pickard, 2011, 2013). It has been repeatedly pointed out that journalism seems to have more difficulty in providing relevant news and that it has failed to engage the public in the type of active participation required for a democracy to function as intended (Van Aelst et al., 2017).

Many hoped that social media would constitute a positive contribution, a revitalization of the public conversation. Initially, much was written about the interactive opportunities on the Internet that could boost people's involvement and engagement in politics and social issues and phenomena such as citizen journalism and participatory journalism, which were highlighted as examples of a promising transformation of both the media landscape and society at large – strikingly often in rather naive and utopian terms (Bruns, 2008; Jenkins, 2006). Although many journalists were initially sceptical of user-generated content (Singer et al., 2011), the opportunities for civic activism, bottom-up democracy and the broadening of public debate were celebrated, at least so far as lip service goes.

Today, a little more than a decade after the "Web 2.0" revolution (O'Reilly, 2005), it sounds quite different. There is more talk of "false news" or disinformation, Russian troll armies and populism than about opinion pluralism, activism and grass roots democracy (Holt, 2018). While previously there were few debaters who advocated restrictions on the possibility of expressing themselves via the Internet and social media, we are today seeing initiatives from various agencies that aim to curb the Internet in order to fight threatening tendencies. In France's parliament, a new law was voted through on 7 June 2018, which aims to ban "fake news" during election campaigns – it makes it possible to get a piece of news appraised as false by a court, whereupon it has to be picked up from the net. In Germany, a new law (NetzDG) came into effect on 1 December 2018, which puts pressure on social media companies to remove hateful material and disinformation – an issue that they still struggle with, but at the same time seems to be too effective in the sense that some content is being blocked because of a difficulty discerning what is actually against the law and what is, for example, satire (Scott & Delcker, 2018). In the US, social media giants have come under fire from many conservative and right-wing actors for being too trigger happy when it comes to blocking or de-platforming content that comes from the right, while looking the other way in other cases (Lewis, 2018). A report commissioned by the Swedish Civil Protection and Emergency Planning Authority (MSB) proposes the following response to, in particular, the negative descriptions from alternative media of the situation in Sweden: "Collaborate with the advertising sector to reduce financial incentives for disinformation" (Colliver, Pomerantsev, Applebaum, & Birdwell, 2018, p. 37). In the media inquiry ordered by the Swedish government (2016), a "democracy clause" was proposed which received sharp criticism from several referral bodies (but the approval of some) and which ultimately did not go through, but which is nevertheless an expression of the same tendency. The democracy clause was intended to grant media support only to actors who are "characterized by the principle of equal value for all and the freedom and dignity of the individual" (p. 331).

These examples illustrate a contemporary tendency to try to find ways to manage and control the unbridled digital information landscape and a jungle of opinions that is often perceived as threatening and hateful. Proposed solutions seem to be more often intended to curtailing many of the aspects with the social media that were initially celebrated. It may appear as the only viable route – but at the same time there are obvious problems associated with such trends that in the long term can create greater challenges for the possibility of free and unbound debate and information sharing. Ultimately, if that is the direction we are heading in, it will be decisive who is in a position to define different actors as false, extreme or hateful, or as someone who does not stand up for the equal value of all humans – and there is a great measure of subjectivity linked to such formulations. They may well be used in ways that we cannot foresee in a future with another political as well as medial balance of power than the one we see today.

Freedom of speech challenged?

Neither the belief in the freedom of expression nor the liberal tradition which has maintained it in modern times is today the obvious point of departure for debates on public discourse and citizenship in democracy. Increasingly, and from various quarters, criticism is heard of phenomena that have previously been defended in the name of freedom of speech. This has been highlighted by John Durham Peters in the book *Courting the abyss – Free speech and the liberal tradition* (2005), but it is a tendency more visible today. The development of the past decades in the media places the old liberal citizens' ideal in new audience and participant situations. In particular, the issue of the presence of evil comes into new light against the background of our present culture's abundance of provocation, vitriol and inflammatory rhetoric. Thoughts on freedom of speech are always associated with the requirement that even the "abyss" must be tolerated – whether we like it or not – and that is the price a free society pays for its freedom. Thus, the tangible presence of evil and generally things that we do not like has been a central theme in the thinking about public communication since ancient times. The classical liberal citizens' ideal required a public conversation where the participants could handle both violations and other things without losing their temper. It also required an audience who understands that even their own toes must run the risk of being trampled without outrage. When Roosevelt was New York's chief of police in the 1890s, Peters reminds us, the German parliamentarian and anti-Semite Hermann Ahlwardt wanted to visit the US. Many in New York wanted to stop him, but Roosevelt chose another way to tackle the problem. He let Ahlwardt keep his speech, protected by 40 police officers – all of whom were Jews. Ahlwardt delivered his anti-Semitic propaganda, framed and protected by a guard of Jewish men. To forbid him to speak would have made him a martyr. Roosevelt's coup demonstrates a way of dealing with opponents that epitomizes an ideal for liberal democratic civilization: To defend the right of people who might hold repulsive views to address the public. The problem is that this requires a willingness for self-sacrifice and an ability for self-abstraction that is quite advanced (Peters, 2005). It means to stoically ignore the hurt personal feelings in order to act on behalf of the hater, assured of everyone's equal right to present their opinions. The rationale can be summarized as an acceptance of the fact that evil ideas must be allowed to spread and that this is a price we must pay to avoid ending up in the even more dangerous situation, in which one starts to set up limits for what can be said and what opinions one may have. In the end, the bad ideas are best dealt with in an open debate where the good ideas and the best arguments will prevail.

But there is also another position, one that might actually be gaining traction in today's polarized debate climate, at least this is the sentiment among many, especially in alternative right-wing media. Instinctively, instead of protecting the right to utter even views that many might find repugnant, many would probably feel like doing what Jake and Elwood did in the movie the Blues Brothers (1980); they drove their Bluesmobile right into the Chicago Nazis' demonstration so they had to jump over the bridge rail, down the canal, uttering "I hate

Nazis!'". This image is perhaps more accurate as an emblem of public discourse today than the example of Roosevelt. In a way, this is
a mode of arguing that perhaps most famously has been articulated
by Herbert Marcuse. Marcuse famously wrote about tolerance in a
book chapter entitled "Repressive tolerance" (Marcuse, 1965). His ar-
gument claims that tolerance of intolerance can be intolerant in itself,
because it serves the interest of those who would themselves impose
oppression upon others. In other words, in a free exchange of ideas, it
is not self-evident that the tolerant ideas would win over the intolerant
ideas, and therefore, he argues, it is necessary take measures in order
to not let that happen (Marcuse, 1965).

As right-wing populist opinions have gained traction throughout
the western world, right-wing alternative media are often described as
a threat to democracy. The focus in public discourse has been, in my
view, disproportionately centered around right-wing extremism, white
supremacy and racism being spread through dubious channels in dark
places on the web. For example, the nebulous alt-right movement has
been much reported on while many still have a problem trying to even
define what it is, and how many people would actually qualify for
membership in such a club. There seems to be an implied link between
populism and extremism similar to the link between a marijuana and
heroin. While it is true that extreme and hateful content is published
online and often targets representatives of minority groups and mainstream media journalists and that especially women are often singled
out and attacked through social media or threatened in other ways, it
is necessary to point out that this is only a part of the story.

In a book about right-wing alternative media, it is impossible to ignore the central question that constantly hovers on the horizon, and that
is debated constantly in most alternative right-wing media I have come
across, but tend to be somewhat avoided in other forums: The perception that free speech is no longer a right that can be counted on and that
political correctness along with hate-speech laws and the interventions
of big tech companies like Twitter, Google and Facebook to demon-
etize and otherwise try to direct traffic away from platforms that are
deemed as harbouring potentially hateful, harmful or false information and opinions. From what I can see, as an observer who has been
lurking on as many right-wing alternative media as I can for the last
five years, many of the successful alternative media outlets on the right
are actually in existence much due to the fact that those who operate
them feel a strong need and even obligation to do something about a
culture which is becoming increasingly oversensitive to provocations
and differing opinions and in which powerful actors can (and do)

intervene in ways that makes a free and open debate very difficult unless you retreat from the major arenas. Especially, there is a perception that attempts to de-platform debaters, scholars and cultural personalities with right-leaning conservative or libertarian opinions are essentially ostracizing large groups of people from a fair chance to participate on today's marketplace of ideas – on university campuses as well as online.

Implications and conclusion

My aim with this book has not been to cover everything that could be said about right-wing alternative media. The research frontier is still too foggy and unclear and the dynamics of public discourse in this time, when things change so quickly that what you wrote yesterday is no longer relevant today, makes it necessary to wait for a few (or more) years to write such a book. Especially, the technological and algorithmic aspects that shape the dynamics of today's media landscape make it difficult methodologically to make systematic observations that are intelligible even for those without degrees in computer science and recognize clear patterns. Instead I have deliberately chosen to focus on what I see are perspectives that are somehow missing or not fully acknowledged in the scholarly as well as the public debate about right-wing alternative media. I will try to summarize these along the lines of the different chapters.

First of all, right-wing alternative media seem to be increasingly relevant to a growing number of people in today's debate. This seems to be linked to political victories in different parts of the world as well. Having said this, I would like to stress that it is necessary to make due distinctions between alternative right-wing media of very different kinds and not lump together all right-wing alternative media but instead study their differences and build theory that is applicable to alternative media of quite different ideological positions. While some are clearly expressions of extremism, radicalism and conspiracy theories, others are merely present during views that they feel are not being treated fairly in mainstream media. In between we find polarizing and provocative expressions, along the same lines, but presented in less agreeable language and imagery that many might find offending but which does not merit labels of extremism. What they do have in common is a critical analysis of present-day public discourse in the way it is being conducted and managed in today's media landscape and a lack of confidence in established media's independence and commitment to the truth. This is actually quite consistent over the whole spectrum – from the more extreme cases to the more conservative and moderate ones.

Why do right-wing alternative media exist?

I have also made the point that it is fruitful to study them *qua* alternative media, since this puts focus on their position as self-perceived correctives of an erring and unjust discourse in established legacy media channels. They exist because there are people on various positions on the right who claim that they are not represented fairly in the major news and views providers, and their audience seek them out because they are looking for media that cover "neglected issues" and provide a platform for diverse voices (Rauch, 2015). This is important to recognize, since this tells us something fundamental about the reason for their existence – seeing themselves as alternatives presupposes something to be an alternative to. This is not to rule out the possibility/fact that there are also powerful organizations that are active in the alternative media scene in order to push certain agendas – this is evident both on the left and the right. In this sense, right-wing alternative media must be understood in *relational* terms, just any other alternative media with different political/ideological leanings.

Are they a threat to the system?

The different ways of positioning themselves as alternatives in relation to the mainstream reveal different reasons and motives for those engaged in the alternative brands. Some are clearly out to undermine the whole system and are not interested in such things as dialogue or gaining acceptance for their views; they are simply too extreme and radical and therefore entrench themselves in their own media sphere, hoping to take over one day in the future. These can clearly be identified as threats to the system – at least in any shape posited by models of democratic governance in which the media serve as an open marketplace of ideas. However, the extreme cases, the clearly anti-system alternative media on the right – such as outspoken Nazi sympathizers and ethno-nationalists – tend to be quite marginal phenomena on the fringes, but every now and then some of them manage to make a lot of noise and provoke established media actors to give them a lot of attention. Polarizing alternative media are media that do not aim to sabotage the system but cause reactions from other actors – because of style or the fact that their views are simply not tolerated and contribute to the dynamics of polarization merely by existing. They are manifestations of tensions within the system but do not constitute a threat. Others yet are acting more out of a frustration with a sense of not being accepted or represented, and seek to gain support for their positions without looking for conflict and within the affordances of free speech according to the rules stipulated by law. Other actors might not like what they say, but this is to be expected and should be possible to handle within a democratic public sphere. Implied here is, of course, a call for a sober look, in public debate as well as in research that does not overemphasize those right-wing alternative media that are most extreme.

Reactions to their existence?

Polarization always requires two poles. It is not, therefore, simply a matter of explaining polarization by pointing to the occurrence of one of them. Indeed, what makes alternative media alternative is a sense of reciprocal animosity between the mainstream and the alternative, especially when it comes to right-wing alternative media. The reactions from some mainstream media, often in concert with established politicians and cultural institutions such as universities, to the rise and success of alternative media like *Breitbart News, Infowars* and parts of the Intellectual Dark Web in the US, or to the *Réinformation media* in France, have often been too simplistic and black and white. As shown in this chapter, the debate about "fake news" for example, a term that more and more people do not want to use, somehow became synonymous to right-wing propaganda attempts (with or without the help from Russia). I am not dismissing the existence of propaganda, the problems of online forums marinated in white supremacy or the alt-right subculture. It is, however, important to point out that some nuance was perhaps lost in the aftermath of Donald Trump's victory in 2016 and that initiatives to fight fake news are blunt instruments and can only accomplish so much, especially in a fragmented and already polarized media environment. In fact, they might also backfire and cause more distrust because the line between fact and opinion is thin, and the labelling of interpretations and views as "false" only confirms already cemented biases against the mainstream media as upholders of establishment truth. There is need for caution when proceeding along such paths.

The future?

It is difficult to talk about the future in relation to the kind of challenges described in this book. The future of media as a platform for news and debate in democratic society is dependent on overarching techno-logical, economic, political and value-related issues. What happens, for example, to established journalism as we know it today if more countries would undergo a shift of the political/ideological climate in a more conservative direction? How are the proposals that are being implemented today to counteract "fake news" and hate speech to influence the possibility for journalists to conduct free and independent investigative reporting of those in power? Perhaps there will not be much difference, but possibly words such as "extremism" and "offensive" are interpreted in slightly different ways than today. What happens if some of the media that today are considered beyond the pale, and as extreme or dangerous in different ways, in a few years would have become more accepted elements of the larger media landscape?

Distrust and hostility towards journalism are most likely here to stay, and it represents to some extent a failure of the large established news providers to convince parts of the population that their news reporting is factual, relevant and impartial. Although trust in the media in general is comparatively strong in some countries, like Sweden (Andersson, Ohlsson, Oscarsson, & Oskarson, 2017), there is no guarantee that this is an eternal state. There are other international comparisons that point in the opposite direction (Ericsson, 2016). The groups of people that have already lost confidence are likely to be difficult to win back (Ladd, 2010). This is especially true when it comes to the sensitive issue of immigration. Since distrust seems more widespread about the question of how journalists have handled issues of social problems related to immigration in many countries, and those individuals who distrust the media to a greater extent lean towards parties that advocate stricter immigration policies, there is reason for self-examination by the journalist. Has there been room for critical discussions and reports about these problems where an immigration critical position is possible? A discussion on such issues has been going on since the 2015 refugee crisis, especially in Sweden, but also in other countries such as Germany, and it is still continuing (see Truedson, 2016; 2017; von Nordheim, Müller & Scheppe. 2019). There are studies that indicate that many media consumers, in Germany, Sweden, Norway and USA, for example, actually experience the established media as more left-wing than what media consumers in other countries do (Ericsson, 2017; von Nordheim, Müller & Scheppe, 2019, In press). The debate will most probably continue.

Another issue that is likely to be more relevant in the future is how long it is justified to talk about some of these media as "alternative" (Rauch, 2016). I previously stressed the importance of this epithet, but I also pointed out that this is by no means a fixed one, especially since the political, social, cultural and media landscape is changing so rapidly. One conceivable scenario is that mainstream journalism incorporates parts of some right-wing alternative media's perspectives, so that certain positions that only existed in the alternative media earlier will in the future also fall within the framework of established journalism.

We can see these tendencies where the *Fox News Channel*, for example, collaborates with *Breitbart News* on some occasions, especially in terms of opinion journalism, where critical perspectives on issues related to immigration are becoming a fairly common and not as controversial element. The same could be said to be happening in Sweden (Bolin, Hinnfors, & Strömbäck, 2016). This would mean a development more in the direction of what it has looked like in other countries such as England, where news reporting just about the immigration issue had a broader spectrum in terms of perspective than Sweden (Berry, Garcia-Blanco, & Moore, 2016). We could call it a broadening of the famous "corridor of opinion" (Oscarsson, 2010).

Further research

I hope that the observations and reflections presented in this book will be useful for public debate as well as future scholarly work on some of the most pressing issues in today's hybrid media landscape (Chadwick, 2013), characterized by polarization and culture wars. I would like to encourage further discussion and research that considers alternative media inspired by diverse political, religious or philosophical ideologies that perceive themselves as correctives to the general discourse of news and views in the most influential mainstream media. Right-wing alternative media are only part of the puzzle, and there is need for studies of similarities and differences between them. In the following I will emphasize a few areas which need to be studied more closely:

First, adopting the proposed notion of anti-systemness points to a need to distinguish between alternative media in different media systems (Mancini, 2013). For example, alternative media in totalitarian or authoritarian states are probably very different compared to alternative media in democratic liberal states. The mainstream media that alternative media position themselves against in countries who already have had a high level of media fragmentation for many years would be of a different nature than the ones that Swedish or American alternative media promises to combat. Here, it becomes obvious that there is a need to acknowledge alternative media from different macro-level perspectives (ideological, cultural, religious and geopolitical), but that the organizational levels, the individuals and the content levels also need to be studied through with the different contexts in mind. International comparative studies of alternative media in different contexts and media systems would be beneficial for furthering our knowledge about the general characteristics of alternative media: It would allow identification of similarities and differences between different media systems.

Second, since debates are raging, especially in the western world, about how to understand the emergence of (at present especially right-wing) alternative media, and their relation to the rise of populism as well as extremism, there is a need for further analysis of the impact of alternative media on the general population in different contexts. As argued in Chapter 3, there is very little information to go on, and there is an apparent risk that their salience is either overestimated or underestimated. The Reuters Institute study has provided an attempt at measuring this (Newman, Fletcher, Kalogeropoulos, Levy, & Kleis Nielsen, 2018), but overall, the research gap here is large, which leaves the field open for speculation.

There is also very little knowledge about the audiences of alternative media and especially their motivations and gratifications. Algorithms that control and suggest content based on our previous click history and the related talk about filter bubbles (Pariser, 2011) have been pointed out as one of the most serious effects that would seem to fuel developments caused by already increasingly fragmented media audiences (Mancini, 2013). However, more research is needed that actually test these assumptions in relation to alternative media consumption, especially in light of other dictums that point to a hybrid media climate, where audience members tend to combine their diet from a variety of sources, rather than just sticking with one (Chadwick, 2013). Furthermore, little is known (at least outside circles of computer programmers) about how the algorithms and various attempts to filter disinformation and hate speech of, for example, Facebook and Google work in relation to steering audiences to or away from different mainstream or alternative media. Since the debate about possible bias in these respects, research that unpacks these complex structures would be beneficial, not only for the advancement of scholarship but also for the general good.

A third aspect that I would like to point out as interesting is the financial aspects of making alternative media work. Alternative media might often not be commercially oriented, but clearly, in many cases they are. Advertising revenue through YouTube is, for example, important to many actors, which is why de-platforming is a heated issue among many actors in right-wing alternative media. Others are instead backed by organizations (or even governments in other countries) who wish to intervene in public discourse for political, cultural, religious or financial reasons. This, of course, plays a crucial role for how they should be analysed and understood.

Lastly, the time of making distinctions between "mainstream" and "alternative" media might be coming to an end or at least this distinction is becoming increasingly difficult to make. I still argue that it is possible to make it, especially since it is arguably a distinction that still is used by and makes sense to many – both users and producers of alternative media. But the fragmentation and hybridization of media consumption – away from the "mass audience" towards ever more polarized and divided media publics – should be studied closely in the near future: When/if right-wing alternative media gain more influence and a larger audience while at the same time becoming more professionalized and also, one might argue, institutionalized as points of reference in public discourse, it is not unthinkable that some also move towards less controversial positions and ways of expressing themselves. It is also not unthinkable that the way representatives of the traditional mainstream might change their reactions and the distance would become less over time. Then it might also be unreasonable for the alternative media to continue identifying as outsiders. If, for example, freshly graduated journalist students seek employment in alternative media, and these also reach out to press unions and ethical committees, for example, and become more recognized players in the traditional realms of established journalism (gaining passes to the White House, participating in conferences arranged by collectives of journalist, etc.) one might ask if the alternative would become more mainstream or if the mainstream (if it still exists) would become more polarized?

Bibliography

Aalberg, T., Esser, F., Reinemann, C., Stromback, J., & De Vreese, C. (2016). *Populist political communication in Europe*. London: Routledge.

Allcott, H., & Gentzkow, M. (2017). Social media and fake news in the 2016 election. *Journal of Economic Perspectives, 31*(2), 211–236. Retrieved from www.aeaweb.org/articles?id=10.1257/jep.31.2.211.

Andersson, U. (2017). Lågt förtroende för rapporteringen om invandring. In L. Truedson (Ed.), *Misstron mot medier* (pp. 17–50). Stockholm: Institutet för mediestudier.

Andersson, U., Ohlsson, J., Oscarsson, H., & Oskarson, M. (2017). Larmar och gör sig till. In U. Andersson, J. Ohlsson, H. Oscarsson & M. Oskarson (Eds.), *Larmar och gör sig till*. Göteborg: SOM-institutet vid Göteborgs universitet.

Arias, F., Åkerman, H., & Karlsson, V. (2016). Grafik: Här finns Nordiska motståndsrörelsen. *Nyheter (Ekot)|Sveriges Radio*. Retrieved January 31, 2019, from https://sverigesradio.se/sida/artikel.aspx?programid=83&artikel=6583295.

Atkinson, J. D., & Leon Berg, S. V. (2012). Narrowmobilization and tea party activism: A study of right-leaning alternative media. *Communication Studies, 63*(5), 519–535. doi:10.1080/10510974.2011.649442.

Attkisson, S. (2017). *The smear: How shady political operatives and fake news control what you see, what you think, and how you vote*. New York, NY: HarperCollins Publishers.

Atton, C. (2002a). *Alternative media*. London: Sage.

Atton, C. (2002b). News cultures and new social movements: Radical journalism and the mainstream media. *Journalism Studies, 3*(4), 491–505.

Atton, C. (2006). Far-right media on the Internet: Culture, discourse and power. *New Media & Society, 8*(4), 573–587. doi:10.1177/1461444806065653.

Atton, C. (2007). Current issues in alternative media research. *Sociology Compass, 1*(1), 17–27. doi:10.1111/j.1751-9020.2007.00005.x.

Atton, C. (2010). Activist media as mainstream model: What can professional journalists learn from Indymedia? In B. Franklin & M. Carlson (Eds.), *Journalists, sources, and credibility* (pp. 73–84). London: Routledge.

82   *Bibliography*

Atton, C. (2015). *The Routledge companion to alternative and community media.* Abingdon: Routledge.
Atton, C., & Wickenden, E. (2005). Sourcing routines and representation in alternative journalism: A case study approach. *Journalism Studies, 6*(3), 347–359.
Bacchetta, P., & Power, M. (2002). *Right-wing women from conservatives to extremists around the world.* New York, NY: Routledge.
Badiou, A. (2005). *Metapolitics.* London: Verso.
Bailey, O., Cammaerts, B., & Carpentier, N. (2007). *Understanding alternative media*: Berkshire: McGraw-Hill Education (UK).
Barbaro, M. (2016, November 09). How did the media – How did we – Get this wrong? *The New York Times.* Retrieved from www.nytimes.com/2016/11/09/podcasts/election-analysis-run-up.html.
Barnidge, M., & Rojas, H. (2014). Hostile media perceptions, presumed media influence, and political talk: Expanding the corrective action hypothesis. *International Journal of Public Opinion Research, 26*(2), 135–156. doi:10.1093/ijpor/edt032.
Bates, T. R. (1975). Gramsci and the Theory of Hegemony. *Journal of the History of Ideas, 36*(2), 351–366.
Beauchamp, Z. (2016, April 4) "Milo Yiannopoulos: Breitbart's Star Provocateur and Trump Champion, Explained," Vox, April 4, 2016. Retrieved from www.vox.com/2016/4/4/11355876/milo-yiannopoulos.
Bernsand, N. (2013). Friend or foe? Contemporary debates on Islam and Muslim immigrants among Swedish identitarians. In T. Hoffmann & G. Larsson (Eds.), *Muslims and the new information and communication technologies* (Vol. 7, pp. 163–189). Dordrecht: Springer Netherlands.
Berry, M., Garcia-Blanco, I., & Moore, K. (2016). Press coverage of the refugee and migrant crisis in the EU: A content analysis of five European countries. UNHCR. Retrieved from www.unhcr.org/56bb369c9.html.
Bertrand, C. J. (2000). *Media ethics & accountability systems.* New Brunswick, NJ: Transaction Publishers.
Binder, E. (2015, 29 November). Keine Lüge: Frauke Petry feiert mit "Pinocchio-Presse". *Der Tagesspiegel.* Retrieved from www.tagesspiegel.de/berlin/bilanz-zum-bundespresseball-keine-luege-frauke-petry-feiert-mit-pinocchio-presse/12652400.html.
Blake, A. (2018, April 3). A new study suggests fake news might have won Donald Trump the 2016 election. *The Washington Post.* Retrieved from https://wapo.st/2q1FMKe?tid=ss_mail&utm_term=.ef0781db21c0.
Blee, K. M., & Creasap, K. A. (2010). Conservative and right-wing movements. *Annual Review of Sociology, 36*(1), 269–286. doi:10.1146/annurev.soc.012809.102602.
Boler, M. (2008). *Digital media and democracy: Tactics in hard times.* Cambridge, London: MIT.
Bolin, N., Hinnfors, J., & Strömbäck, J. (2016). Invandring på ledarsidorna i svensk nationell dagspress 2010–2015. In *Migrationen i medierna: men det får en väl inte prata om* (1st ed., pp. 192–211). Stockholm: Institutet för mediestudier. Retrieved from http://urn.kb.se/resolve?urn=urn:nbn:se:miun:diva-27780.

Borgs, M. (2015). Alternativa medier vs public service. Retrieved from https://medium.com/@martinborgs/alternativa-medier-public-service-ea3110e384ec.

Bossetta, M. (2012). *Cultural racism without race: An exploratory insight into the discrimination and self-perception of the Sweden democrats* (Master of Arts). Lund University, Lund.

Bowman-Grieve, L. (2009). Exploring "stormfront": A virtual community of the radical right. *Studies in Conflict & Terrorism, 32*(11), 989–1007. doi:10.1080/10576100903259951.

Brants, K., de Vreese, C., Möller, J., & Van Praag, P. (2009). The real spiral of cynicism? Symbiosis and mistrust between politicians and journalists. *The International Journal of Press/Politics.*

Brown, C. (2009). White supremacist discourse on the Internet and the construction of whiteness ideology. *Howard Journal of Communications, 20*(2), 189–208. doi:10.1080/10646170902869544.

Brügger, N. (2009). Website history and the website as an object of study. *New Media & Society, 11*(1–2), 115–132. doi:10.1177/1461444808099574.

Bruns, A. (2008). *Blogs, wikipedia, second life, and beyond: From production to produsage.* New York: Peter Lang.

Cammaerts, B. (2009). Radical pluralism and free speech in online public spaces: The case of North Belgian extreme right discourses. *International Journal of Cultural Studies, 12*(6), 555–575.

Capoccia, G. (2002). Anti-system parties: A conceptual reassessment. *Journal of Theoretical Politics, 14*(1), 9–35.

Cappella, J. N. (2002). Cynicism and social trust in the new media environment. *Journal of Communication, 52*(1), 229–241.

Cappella, J. N., & Jamieson, K. H. (1996). News frames, political cynicism, and media cynicism. *Annals of the American Academy of Political and Social Science, 546*, 71–84. doi:10.2307/1048171.

Carey, J. W. (2007). A short history of journalism for journalists: A proposal and essay. *Harvard International Journal of Press/Politics, 12*(1), 3–16. doi:10.1177/1081180X06297603.

Carpentier, N. (2011). *Media and participation: A site of ideological-democratic struggle.* Bristol: Intellect Books.

Chadwick, A. (2013). *The hybrid media system: Politics and power.* New York, NY: Oxford University Press.

Chomsky, N. (1997). What makes mainstream media mainstream. *Z magazine, 10*(10), 17–23.

Colliver, C., Pomerantsev, P., Applebaum, A., & Birdwell, J. (2018). Smearing Sweden international influence campaigns in the 2018 Swedish election. London. Retrieved from www.isdglobal.org/wpcontent/uploads/2018/10/Sweden_Report_October_2018.pdf.

Conboy, M. (2004). *Journalism: A critical history.* London: Sage.

Couldry, N. (2003). Digital divide or discursive design? On the emerging ethics of information space. *Ethics and Information Technology, 5*(2), 89–97.

Coyer, K., Dowmunt, T., & Fountain, A. (2007). *The alternative media handbook.* London: Routledge.

84 Bibliography

CPJ. (2018). "58 Journalists Killed in Russia between 1992 and 2018 / Motive Confirmed". Committee to protect journalists. Retrieved from https://cpj. org/data/killed/europe/russia/?status=Killed&motiveConfirmed% 5B%5D=Confirmed&type%5B%5D=Journalist&cc_fips%5B% 5D=RS&startyear=1992&end_year=201 &group_by=location.

Dahlgren, P., & Alvares, C. (2016). Populism, extremism, and media: Mapping an uncertain terrain. *European Journal of Communication.*, *31*(1), 46–57. doi:10.1177/0267323115614485.

Darity Jr., W. A. (Ed.). (2008, January 22). *Right wing* (2nd ed., IB, Vol. 7, pp. 247–248). Detroit, MI: Macmillan Reference USA. Retrieved from http://link.galegroup.com/apps/doc/CX3045302284/GVRL?u=vaxuniv& sid=GVRL&xid=81ad9c49.

De Benoist, A., & Champetier, C. (1999). *The French new right in the year 2000.* New York: Telos.

De Koster, W., & Houtman, D. (2008). Stormfront is like a second home to me. *Information, Communication & Society, 11*(8), 1155–1176. doi:10.1080/ 13691180802266665.

Deland, M., Hertzberg, F., & Hvitfeldt, T. (2010). *Det vita fältet: samtida forskning om högerextremism.* Uppsala: Historiska institutionen, Uppsala universitet.

Demker, M. (2012). *Positiv attityd till invandring trots mobilisering av invandringsmotstånd. i Lennart Weibull, Henrik Oscarsson och Annika Bergström, red, I framtidens skugga.* Göteborg: Göteborgs universitet, SOM-institutet.

Doudaki, V., Carpentier, N., & Christidis, Y. (2015, October 23–24). *Technological struggles in community media.* Paper presented at the 'Theorizing Media and Conflict' Workshop, European Association of Social Anthropologists, Vienna.

Downey, J., & Fenton, N. (2003). New media, counter publicity and the public sphere. *New Media & Society, 5*(2), 185–202. doi:10.1177/1461444803005002 003.

Downing, J. D. H. (2003). Audiences and readers of alternative media: The absent lure of the virtually unknown. *Media, Culture & Society, 25*(5), 625–645. doi:10.1177/01634437030255004.

Downing, J. D. H., & Ford, T. V. (2001). *Radical media: Rebellious communication and social movements.* Thousand Oaks, CA: Sage.

Ekman, M., & Widholm, A. (2014). Politicians as media producers. *Journalism Practice, 9*(1), 78–91. doi:10.1080/17512786.2014.928467.

Ellinas, A. A. (2010). *The media and the far right in Western Europe.* Cambridge: Cambridge University Press.

Ericsson, A. (2017) Mitt försök att förstå misstron mot medier. In L. Truedson (Ed.), *Misstron mot medier* (pp. 166–176). Stockholm: Institutet för mediestudier.

Faris, R., Roberts, H., Etling, B., Bourassa, N., Zuckerman, E., & Benkler, Y. (2017). Partisanship, propaganda, and disinformation: online media and the 2016 US presidential election. Berkman Klein Center for Internet &

Society Research Paper. Retreived from http://nrs.harvard.edu/urn-3:HUL. InstRepos:33759251.

Fenton, N. (2008). New media, politics and resistance. In M. Pajnik & J. D. H. Downing (Eds.), *Alternative media and the politics of resistance perspectives and challenges* (pp. 61–81). Ljubljana: Peace Institute.

Fernquist, J., Kaati, L., Akrami, N., Cohen, K., & Schroeder, R. (2018). *Botar och det svenska valet. Automatiserade konton, deras budskap och omfattning.* Stockholm. Retrieved from www.foi.se/rapportsammanfattning?reportNo= FOI MEMO 6458.

Fichtelius, E. (2016). *Vad är en nyhet: och 100 andra jätteviktiga frågor/Erik Fichtelius.* Stockholm: Langenskiöld.

Fraser, N. (1990). Rethinking the public sphere: A contribution to the critique of actually existing democracy. *Social Text, 1990* (25/26), 56–80.

Friman, C. (2018, January). Högerspöket. *Magasinet Filter* #60. Retrieved from https://magasinetfilter.se/reportage/hogerspoket/.

Frye, C. E. (1966). Carl Schmitt's concept of the political. *The Journal of Politics, 28*(04), 818–830.

Fulgoni, G. M., Lipsman, A., & Davidsen, C. (2016). The power of political advertising: Lessons for practitioners: How data analytics, social media, and creative strategies shape US presidential election campaigns. *Journal of Advertising Research, 56*(3), 239–244.

Fuller, D. [*Rebel Wisdom*]. (2018, February 1). "A glitch in the matrix" – Jordan Peterson, the Intellectual Dark Web & the mainstream media [Video file]. Retrieved from https://youtu.be/trhTbEs2GGE.

Griffin, R. (2000). Between metapolitics and apoliteia: The Nouvelle Droite's strategy for conserving the fascist vision in the 'interregnum'. *Modern & Contemporary France, 8*(1), 35–53. doi:10.1080/096394800113349.

Guess, A., Nyhan, B., & Reifler, J. (2018). Selective exposure to misinformation: Evidence from the consumption of fake news during the 2016 US presidential campaign. *European Research Council*, 1–49.

Gutsche Jr., R. E. (Ed.). (2018). *The Trump presidency, journalism, and democracy.* New York, NY: Routledge.

Gourarie, C. (2016). How the 'alt-right' checkmated the media. *Columbia Journalism Review.* Retrieved from www.cjr.org/analysis/alt_right_media_clinton_trump.php.

Grafstein, R. (2018). The problem of polarization. *Public Choice, 176*(1–2), 315–340. doi:10.1007/s11127-018-0547-z.

Gramsci, A., & Buttigieg, J. A. (1992). *Prison notebooks* (Vol. 2). New York: Columbia University Press.

Habermas, J. (1989). *The structural transformation of the public sphere: An inquiry into a category of bourgeois society. Studies in contemporary German social thought.* Cambridge: MIT Press.

Hackett, R. A., & Gurleyen, P. (2015). Beyond the binaries? Alternative media and objective journalism. In C. Atton (Ed.), *The Routledge companion to alternative and community media* (pp. 54–65). London: Routledge.

86   Bibliography

Haller, A., & Holt, K. (2018). Paradoxical populism: How PEGIDA relates to mainstream and alternative media. *Information, Communication & Society*. doi:10.1080/1369118X.2018.1449882.

Haller, A., Holt, K. & de la Brosse, R. (2019). The "other" alternatives: Political right-wing alternative media. *Journal of Alternative and Community Media*, *4*(1), 1–9.

Haller, M. (2017). Die "Flüchtlingskrise" in den Medien. Tagesaktueller Journalismus zwischen Meinung und Information. Eine Studie der Otto Brenner Stiftung. Retrieved from www.otto-brennerstiftung.de/fileadmin/user_data/stiftung/Aktuelles/AH93/AH_93_Haller_Web.pdf.

Hallin, D. C. (1989). *The uncensored war: The media and Vietnam*. Berkeley: University of California Press.

Harcup, T. (2005). "I'm doing this to change the world": Journalism in alternative and mainstream media. *Journalism Studies*, *6*(3), 361–374.

Harcup, T. (2011). Alternative journalism as active citizenship. *Journalism*, *12*(1), 15–31. doi:10.1177/1464884910385191.

Harvard, J. (2006). *En helig allmännelig opinion: Föreställningar om offentlighet och legitimitet i svensk riksdagsdebatt 1848–1919* (PhD dissertation). Historiska studier, Umeå.

Hedman, F., Sivnert, F., & Howard, P. N. (2018). *News and political information consumption in Sweden: Mapping the 2018 Swedish general election on Twitter*. Oxford. Retrieved from http://comprop.oii.ox.ac.uk/wp-content/uploads/sites/93/2018/09/Hedman-et-al-2018.pdf.

Hedman, U. (2018). Journalister och alternativa journalister på Twitter. In L. I Nord, M. Grusell, N. Bolin & K. Falasca (Eds.), *Snabbtänkt: Reflektioner från valet 2018 av ledande forskare* (s. 85). Sundsvall: Demicom.

Hellström, A., & Nilsson, T. (2010). 'We are the good guys': Ideological positioning of the nationalist party Sverigedemokraterna in contemporary Swedish politics. *Ethnicities*, *10*(1), 55–76. doi:10.1177/1468796809354214.

Herman, E. S., & Chomsky, N. (1988). *Manufacturing consent: The political economy of the mass media*. London: Vintage.

Hogan, B. (2010). The presentation of self in the age of social media: Distinguishing performances and exhibitions online. *Bulletin of Science, Technology & Society*, *30*(6), 377–386.

Holt, K. (2015). The religious dimension of Kierkegaard's media criticism. 'Authentic faith' vs. 'the phantom public'. In V. Khroul (Ed.), *Mediatization of religion: Historical and functional perspectives* (pp. 30–49). Moscow: Faculty of Journalism, Lomonosov Moscow State University.

Holt, K. (2016a). "Alternativmedier"? En intervjustudie om mediekritik och mediemisstro. In L. Truedson (Ed.), *Migrationen i medierna – Men det får en väl inte prata om?* (pp. 113–149). Stockholm: Institutet för mediestudier.

Holt, K. (2016b). Journalistik bortom redaktionerna? In Westlund (red.), *Människorna, medierna & marknaden* (s. 403–428). Medieutredningens forskningsantologi om en demokrati i förändring. SOU 2016:30. Stockholm: Wolters Kluwer.

Holt, K. (2017, September 11–12). Media distrust: A left-wing or right-wing specialty?: Historical perspectives on today's debate about populism and the media. In *Perspectives on Right-Wing Populism and the Media: Scholarship, Journalism, Civil Society*. Munich: Center for Advanced Studies (CAS), LMU Munich.

Holt, K. (2018). Alternative media and the notion of anti-systemness: Towards an analytical framework journal of media and communication (invited contribution for special issue Vol 6, Issue 4: News and participation through and beyond proprietary platforms in an age of social medias. Edited by Oscar Westlund and Mats Ekström). *Media and Communication, 6*(4), 49–57. doi:10.17645/mac.v6i4.1467.

Holt, K., & de la Brosse, R. (2017). Médias antisystèmes et tentatives de 'réinformation' du public: Regards croisés sur les expériences suédoise et française. Les journalistes dans le débat démocratique Théofraste Network, Tunis, Tunisia 23–25 October 2017.

Holt, K., & Haller, A. (2016). *The populist communication paradox of PEGIDA: Between "Lying Press" and journalistic sources*. Paper presented at the 66th annual ICA conference "communicating with power". Fukuoka, Japan, 9–13 June. Preconference: Populism in, by, and Against the Media.

Holt, K., & Haller, A. (2017). What does 'Lügenpresse' mean? Expressions of media distrust on PEGIDA's Facebook pages. *Politik, 20*(4), 16–42.

Holt, K., & Karlsson, M. (2014). Om journalistikens existentiella kris – behövs verkligen journalister när Vem von Helst kan bli publicist? *IKAROS, 11*(3–4), 5–7.

Holt, K., & Rinaldo, M. (2014). *Exploring the dark side of participatory online media: Online participation, identitarian discourse and media criticism at Metapedia.org*. Paper presented at JSS-ECREA 2014 Conference: Journalism in Transition: Crisis or Opportunity? Thessaloniki, Greece.

Holt, K., & von Krogh, T. (2010). The citizen as media critic in periods of media change. *Observatorio (OBS*), 4*(4). Retrieved from http://obs.obercom.pt/index.php/obs/article/view/432.

Holt, K., Figenshou, T., & Frischlich, L. (2019). Key dimensions of alternative news media. *Digital Journalism*. doi: 10.1080/21670811.2019.1625715.

Hooghe, L., Marks, G., & Wilson, C. J. (2002). Does left/right structure party positions on european integration?, *35*(8), 965–989. https://doi.org/10. 1177/001041402236310.

Howard, P. N., & Bradshaw, S. (2017, May 4). Junk news and bots during the French presidential election: What are French voters sharing over Twitter in round two? *COMPROP Data Memo/2017.4*.

Hughey, M. W., & Daniels, J. (2013). Racist comments at online news sites: A methodological dilemma for discourse analysis. *Media, Culture & Society, 35*(3), 332–347. doi:10.1177/0163443712472089

Iost, D. (2012). L'extrême droite allemande: une stratégie de communication moderne. *Hérodote* (1), 60–76.

Jackob, N. G. E. (2010). No alternatives? The relationship between perceived media dependency, use of alternative information sources, and general trust in mass media. *International Journal of Communication, 4*, 18. 589–607.

Jagers, J., & Walgrave S. (2007). Populism as political communication style: An empirical study of political parties' discourse in Belgium. *European Journal of Political Research, 46*(3): 319–345.

Jahn, D. (2011). Conceptualizing left and right in comparative politics: Towards a deductive approach. *Party Politics, 17*(6), 745–765. doi:10.1177/1354068810380091.

Jamieson, K. H., & Cappella, J. N. (2008). *Echo chamber: Rush Limbaugh and the conservative media establishment.* Oxford: Oxford University Press.

Jenkins, H. (2006). *Convergence culture: Where old and new media collide.* New York: New York University Press.

Karlsson, M., & Holt, K. (2016). Journalism on the Web. In J. F. Nussbaum (Ed.), *Oxford research encyclopedia of communication.* Oxford: Oxford University Press.

Kaun, A. (2014). 'I really don't like them!' – Exploring citizens' media criticism. *European Journal of Cultural Studies, 17*(5), 489–506. doi:10.1177/1367549413515259.

Kenix, L. J. (2011). *Alternative and mainstream media: The converging spectrum.* London: A&C Black.

Kierkegaard, S., & Hannay, A. (2001). *A literary review: Two ages, a novel by the author of a story of everyday life*, published by J.L. Heiberg, Copenhagen, Reitzel, 1845. London: Penguin.

Knigge, P. (1998). The ecological correlates of right-wing extremism in Western Europe. *European Journal of Political Research, 34*(2), 249–279. doi:10.1023/A:1006953714624.

Knödler-Bunte, E., Lennox, S., & Lennox, F. (1975). The proletarian public sphere and political organization: An analysis of Oskar Negt and Alexander Kluge's the public sphere and experience. *New German Critique, 1*(4), 51–75.

Kobayashi, T., & Ikeda, K. I. (2009). Selective exposure in political web browsing: Empirical verification of 'cyber-balkanization' in Japan and the USA. *Information, Communication & Society, 12*(6), 929–953. doi:10.1080/13691180802158490.

Kováts, E. (2018). Questioning consensuses: Right-wing populism, anti-populism, and the threat of 'gender ideology'. *Sociological Research Online, 23*(2), 528–538. doi:10.1177/1360780418764735.

Krämer, B. (2014). Media populism: A conceptual clarification and some theses on its effects. *Communication Theory, 24*(1), 42–60.

Krämer, B. (2017). Populist online practices: The function of the Internet in right-wing populism. *Information, Communication & Society, 20*(9), 1293–1309.

Krämer, B. (2018). Populism, media, and the form of society. *Communication Theory, 28*(4), 444–465.

Ladd, J. M. (2010). *Why Americans distrust the news media and how it matters.* Princeton University Press. doi:10.1080/10584609.2012.722512.

Larsson, A. O. (2015). Going viral? Comparing parties on social media during the 2014 Swedish election. *Convergence: The International Journal of Research into New Media Technologies.* doi:10.1177/1354856515577891.

Lawrence, R. G., & Boydstun, A. E. (2017). What we should really be asking about media attention to Trump. *Political Communication, 34*(1), 150–153. doi:10.1080/10584609.2016.1262700.

Lazer, D. M. J., Baum, M. A., Benkler, Y., Berinsky, A. J., Greenhill, K. M., Menczer, F., ... Rothschild, D. (2018). The science of fake news. *Science, 359*(6380), 1094–1096.

Leung, D. K., & Lee, F. L. (2014). Cultivating an active online counterpublic examining usage and political impact of Internet alternative media. *The International Journal of Press/Politics, 19*(3), 340–359.

Lewis, R. (2018). Alternative influence: Broadcasting the reactionary right on YouTube. *Data & Society*. Retrieved from https://datasociety.net/research/media-manipulation.

Lievrouw, L. (2011). *Alternative and activist new media*. Malden, MA: Polity.

Lippmann, W. (1922). *Public opinion*. London: Allen & Unwin.

Lundell, P. (2002). *Pressen i provinsen: från medborgerliga samtal till modern opinionsbildning 1750–1850*. Lund: Nordic Academic Press.

Lundell, P. (2008). The medium is the message – The media history of the press. *Media History, 14*(1), 1–16.

Lundström, G., Rydén, P., & Sandlund, E. (red.) (2001). *Den svenska pressens historia. 3, Det moderna Sveriges spegel (1897–1945)*. Stockholm: Ekerlid.

Lynskey, D. (2018, February 7). How dangerous is Jordan B Peterson, the right wing professor who 'hit a hornets' nest'? *The Guardian*. Retrieved from www.theguardian.com/science/2018/feb/07/how-dangerous-is-jordan-b-peterson-the-rightwing-professor-who-hit-a-hornets-nest.

Major, M. (2015). Conservative consciousness and the press: The institutional contribution to the idea of the 'liberal media' in right-wing discourse. *Critical Sociology, 41*(3), 483–491.

Malloy, T., & Rubenstein, P. S. (2018). *U.S. voters dislike Trump almost 2-1, Quinnipiac University National Poll finds; Media is important to democracy, 65% of voters say*. Quinnipiac: Quinnipiac University. Retrieved Hämtad från, from www.facebook.com/quinnipiacpoll.

Mancini, P. (2013). Media fragmentation, party system, and democracy. *International Journal of Press/Politics, 18*(1), 43–60. doi:10.1177/1940161212458200.

Marcuse, H. (1965). Repressive tolerance. In R. P. Wolff, J. Barrington Moore & H. Marcuse (Eds.), *A critique of pure tolerance* (pp. 81–117). Boston, MA: Beacon Press.

Mattsson, C. (2018). *Nordiska motståndsrörelsens ideologi, propaganda och livsåskådning*. Göteborg: Segerstedtinstitutet. Retrieved from https://segerstedtinstitutet.gu.se/digitalAssets/1693/1693644_rapport7-si.pdf.

Mazzoleni, G. (2008). Populism and the media. In D. Albertazzi & D. McDonnell (Eds.), *Twenty-first century populism. The spectre of Western European Democracy* (pp. 49–64). New York, NY: Palgrave Macmillan.

Mazzoleni, G. (2014). Mediatization and political populism. In F. Esser & J. Strömbäck (Eds.), *Mediatization of politics: Understanding the transformation of western democracies* (p. 42). Basingstoke: Palgrave MacMillan.

Meddaugh, P. M., & Kay, J. (2009). Hate speech or "reasonable racism?" The other in stormfront. *Journal of Mass Media Ethics, 24*(4), 251–268. doi:10.1080/08900520903320936.

Medders, R. B., & Metzger, M. J. (2018). The role of news brands and leads in exposure to political information on the Internet. *Digital Journalism, 6*(5), 599–618. doi:10.1080/21670811.2017.1320770.

Meraz, S. (2009). Is there an elite hold? Traditional media to social media agenda setting influence in blog networks. *Journal of Computer-Mediated Communication, 14*(3), 682–707. doi:10.1111/j.1083–6101.2009.01458.x.

Meraz, S. (2011). The fight for 'how to think': Traditional media, social networks, and issue interpretation. *Journalism, 12*(1), 107–127.

Mouffe, C. (2013, September 16). Five minutes with Chantal Mouffe: "Most countries in Europe are in a post-political situation". Retrieved December 1, 2014, from http://bit.ly/18midhv.

Mudde, C. (2014). Fighting the system? Populist radical right parties and party system change. *Party Politics, 20*(2), 217–226. doi:10.1177/1354068813519968.

Mullen, A. (2010). Twenty years on: The second-order prediction of the Herman-Chomsky propaganda model. *Media, Culture & Society, 32*(4), 673–690.

Mullen, A., & Klaehn, J. (2010). The Herman–Chomsky propaganda model: A critical approach to analysing mass media behaviour. *Sociology Compass, 4*(4), 215–229.

Nagle, A. (2017). *Kill all normies: Online culture wars from 4chan and Tumblr to Trump and the alt-right.* Hants: John Hunt Publishing.

Nash, C. (2016, 10 November). Breitbart Beats NY Times, CNN, and Fox News for Election Day Facebook Engagement. *Breitbart.* Retrieved from www.breitbart.com/tech/2016/11/10/breitbart-beats-ny-times-cnn-fox-news-election-day-facebook-engagement/.

Negt, O., & Kluge, A. (1972). *Public sphere and experience: Towards an analysis of the bourgeois and proletarian public sphere.* Minneapolis: University of Minnesota Press.

Negt, O., Kluge, A., & Kluge, A. (1972). *Öffentlichkeit und Erfahrung: zur Organisationsanalyse von bürgerlicher und proletarischer Öffentlichkeit.* Suhrkamp.

Nehamas, A. (1988). Plato and the mass media. *The Monist, 71*(2), 214–234. doi:10.2307/27903079.

Newman, N., Fletcher, R., Kalogeropoulos, A., Levy, D. A. L., & Kleis Nielsen, R. (2018). *Reuters Institute Digital News Report 2018.* Oxford: Reuters Institute. Retrieved from http://media.digitalnewsreport.org/wp-content/uploads/2018/06/DNR_2018-FINAL_WEB.pdf?x89475.

Nilsson, M. L. (2017). *Journalisternas trygghetsundersökning.* Göteborg: JMG, Göteborgs universitet.

Nordfront.se (2017). Största nationella samlingen i Göteborg i modern tid| Nordfront.se. Retrieved January 31, 2019, from www.nordfront.se/storsta-nationella-samlingen-goteborg-modern-tid.smr.

Nordheim, G. v., Müller, H., & Scheppe, M. (2019). Young, free and biased: A comparison of mainstream and right-wing media coverage of the 2015–16 refugee crisis in German newspapers. *Journal of Alternative and Community Media, 4*(1), 38–57.

Nygaard, S. (2019). The appearance of objectivity: How immigration-critical alternative media report the news. *Journalism Practice*. Published ahead of print February 2019. doi:10.1080/17512786.2019.1577697.

Ohlsson, J. (2014). Fading support for the Swedish press support. *Journal of Media Business Studies, 11*(1), 39–60. doi:10.1080/16522354.2014.11073575.

Oja, S., & Mral, B. (2013). The Sweden democrats came in from the cold: How the debate about allowing the SD into media arenas shifted between 2002 and 2010. In R. Wodak, M. KhosraviNik & B. Mral (Eds.), *Right-wing populism in Europe: Politics and discourse* (pp. 277–292). London: Bloomsbury Academic.

O'Reilly, T. (2005, September 30). What is Web 2.0? design patterns and business models for the next generation of software. Retrieved from http://oreilly.com/web2/archive/what-is-web-20.html.

Oscarsson, H. E. (2013). Väljare är inga dumbommar. Retrieved from https://politologerna.wordpress.com/2013/12/10/valjare-ar-inga-dumbommar/.

Pajnik, M., & Downing, J. D. (2008). *Alternative media and the politics of resistance*. Ljubljana: Peace Institute.

Panizza, F. (2005). *Populism and the mirror of democracy*. London: Verso.

Pariser, E. (2011). *The filter bubble: What the Internet is hiding from you.* Penguin UK.

Paternotte, D., & Kuhar, R. (2018). Disentangling and locating the "global right": Anti-gender campaigns in Europe. *Politics and Governance, 6*(3), 6–19. doi:10.17645/pag.v6i3.1557.

Patterson, T. E. (2016). News coverage of the 2016 general election: How the press failed the voters. Harvard University, John F. Kennedy School of Government.

Patterson, T. E. (2017). *News coverage of Donald Trump's first 100 days.* Harvard University, John F. Kennedy School of Government.

Penney, J., & Dadas, C. (2014). (Re)Tweeting in the service of protest: Digital composition and circulation in the Occupy Wall Street movement. *New Media & Society, 16*(1), 74–90.

Perloff, R. M. (2015). A three-decade retrospective on the hostile media effect. *Mass Communication and Society*, 1–29. doi:10.1080/15205436.2015.1051234.

Peters, J. D. (2005). *Courting the Abyss: Free speech and the liberal tradition.* Chicago, IL: University of Chicago Press.

Pickard, V. (2011). Revisiting the road not taken: A social democratic vision of the press. In R. McChesney & V. Pickard (Eds.), *Will the last reporter please turn out the lights: The collapse of journalism and what can be done to fix it* (pp. 174–184). New York: The New Press.

Pickard, V. (2013). Social democracy or corporate libertarianism? Conflicting media policy narratives in the wake of market failure. *Communication Theory, 23*(4), 336–355. doi:10.1111/comt.12021.

Rappeport, A. (2015, August 11). From the right, a new slur for G.O.P. Candidates. *The New York Times*.

Rauch, J. (2007). Activists as interpretive communities: Rituals of consumption and interaction in an alternative media audience. *Media, Culture & Society, 29*(6), 994–1013.

Rauch, J. (2015). Exploring the alternative–mainstream dialectic: What "alternative media" means to a hybrid audience. *Communication, Culture & Critique, 8*(1), 124–143. doi:10.1111/cccr.12068.

Rauch, J. (2016). Are there still alternatives? Relationships between alternative media and mainstream media in a converged environment. *Sociology Compass, 10*(9), 756–767. doi:10.1111/soc4.12403.

Right Wing. (2008). In W. A. Darity, Jr. (Ed.), *International Encyclopedia of the Social Sciences* (2nd ed., Vol. 7, pp. 247–248). Detroit, MI: Macmillan Reference USA. Retrieved from http://link.galegroup.com.proxy.lnu.se/apps/doc/CX3045302284/GVRL?u=vaxuniv&sid=GVRL&xid=81ad9c49.

Romancini, R., & Castilho, F. (2019). Strange fruit: The rise of Brazil's 'new right-wing' and the Non-Partisan School Movement. *Journal of Alternative and Community Media, 4*(1), 16.

Rydgren, J. (2005). *Radical right-wing populism in Sweden and Denmark.* Paper presented at The Centre for the Study of European Politics and Society, 2005 Seminars.

Sartori, G. (2005). *Parties and party systems: A framework for analysis.* Colchester: ECPR Press.

Schneider, S. M, & Foot, K. A. (2004). The web as an object of study. *New Media & Society, 6*(1), 114–122.

Scott, M., & Delcker, J. (2018, January 6). Free speech vs. censorship in Germany: New rules on online hate speech cause problems for Internet giants. *Politico.* Retrieved from www.politico.eu/article/germany-hate-speech-netzdg-facebook-youtube-google-twitter-free-speech/.

Scruton, R. (2002). *The meaning of conservatism.* Chicago, IL: St. Augustine Press.

Shin, J., & Thorson, K. (2017). Partisan selective sharing: The biased diffusion of fact-checking messages on social media. *Journal of Communication, 67*(2), 233–255.

Shoemaker, P. J. (1984). Media treatment of deviant political groups. *Journalism Quarterly, 61*(1), 66–82. doi:10.1177/107769908406100109.

Shoemaker, P. J., & Reese, S. D. (2014). *Mediating the message in the 21st century: A media sociological perspective.* New York, NY: Routledge.

Singer, J. B. (2013). The ethical implications of an Elite Press. *Journal of Mass Media Ethics, 28*(3), 203–216. doi:10.1080/08900523.2013.802163.

Singer, J. B., Domingo, D., Heinonen, A., Hermida, A., Paulussen, S., Quandt, T., … & Vujnovic, M. (2011). *Participatory journalism: Guarding open gates at online newspapers.* Hoboken, NJ: John Wiley & Sons.

Sköld, J. (2018). Avpixlats huvudman nekas medlemskap i Publicistklubben, Aftonbladet. Retrieved April 2, 2013, from www.aftonbladet.se/nyheter/article16527633.ab.

Suk, V. (2017, April 1). Alternativmedia farligare än IS-terrorister – för vem? *Nya Tider.* Retrieved from www.nyatider.nu/alternativmedia-farligare-an-is-terrorister-for-vem/.

Sunstein, C. R. (2007). *Republic.com 2.0*. Princeton, NJ: Princeton University Press.

Taguieff, P.-A. (1998). Populismes et antipopulismes: le choc des argumentations. *Mots, 55*(1), 5–26.

Tateo, L. (2005). The Italian extreme right on-line network: An exploratory study using an integrated social network analysis and content analysis approach. *Journal of Computer-Mediated Communication, 10*(2), doi:10.1111/j.1083–6101.2005.tb00247.x.

The Local (2018, November 8). "Crawl back under your rock". Swedish foreign minister tells Canadian professor Jordan B Peterson. Retrieved January 13, 2019, from www.thelocal.se/20181108/crawl-back-under-your-rock-swedish-foreign-minister-tells-canadian-professor-jordan-peterson.

Tripodi, F. (2018). Searching for alternative facts: analyzing scriptural inference in conservative news practices. Retrieved from https://datasociety.net/wp-content/uploads/2018/05/Data_Society_Searching-for-Alternative-Facts_FINAL-5.pdf.

Truedson, L. (2016). *Migrationen i medierna–men det får en väl inte prata om.* Stockholm: Institutet för mediestudier.

Truedson, L. (2017). *Misstron mot medier.* Stockholm: Institutet för mediestudier.

Trump, D. J. [realDonaldTrump]. (2018, October 30). CNN and others in the fake news business keep purposely and inaccurately reporting that i said the "Media is the en …". https://t.co/RQt2MhFTlr [Tweet]. Retrieved from https://twitter.com/realDonaldTrump/status/1057059603605831680.

Tsfati, Y. (2003). Media skepticism and climate of opinion perception. *International Journal of Public Opinion Research, 15*(1), 65–82.

Tsfati, Y., & Cohen, J. (2005). Democratic consequences of hostile media perceptions: The case of Gaza settlers. *The Harvard International Journal of Press/Politics, 10*(4), 28–51.

Uldam, J., & Vestergaard, A. (2015). *Civic engagement and social media: Political participation beyond protest.* Basingstoke: Palgrave Macmillan.

Vallone, R. P., Ross, L., & Lepper, M. R. (1985). The hostile media phenomenon: Biased perception and perceptions of media bias in coverage of the Beirut massacre. *Journal of personality and social psychology,* 49(3), 577–585.

Van Aelst, P., Strömbäck, J., Aalberg, T., Esser, F., de Vreese, C., Matthes, J., & Stanyer, J. (2017). Political communication in a high-choice media environment: A challenge for democracy? *Annals of the International Communication Association, 41*(1), 3–27. doi:10.1080/23808985.2017.1288551.

Vargo, C. J., Guo, L., & Amazeen, M. A. (2017). The agenda-setting power of fake news: A big data analysis of the online media landscape from 2014 to 2016. *New Media & Society,* 2028–2049. doi:10.1177/1461444817712086.

Viereck, P. (2003). Metapolitics revisited. *Humanitas, 16*(2), 48–75.

Viereck, P. (2004). *Metapolitics: From Wagner and the German romantics to Hitler.* New Brunswick, NJ: Transaction Publishers.

Vos, T. P., Craft, S., & Ashley, S. (2011). New media, old criticism: Bloggers' press criticism and the journalistic field. *Journalism, 13*(7), 850–868. doi:10.1177/1464884911421705.

Wåg, M. (2010). Nationell kulturkamp – från vit makt musik till metapolitik. In M. Deland, F. Hertzberg & T. Hvitfeldt (Eds.), *Det vita fältet. Samtida forskning om högerextremism* (pp. 97–126). Uppsala: Dept. of History, Uppsala University.

Weibull, L. (2017). Synen på sanning i nyheterna. In L. Truedson (Ed.), *Misstron mot medier* (pp. 136–165). Stockholm: Institutet för mediestudier.

Weiss, B. (2018, August 5). Opinion: Meet the Renegades of the Intellectual Dark Web. An Alliance of Heretics is Making an End Run around the Mainstream Conversation. Should We be Listening? *The New York Times.* Retrieved from www.nytimes.com/2018/05/08/opinion/intellectual-dark-web.html.

Wodak, R., KhosraviNik, M., & Mral, B. (2013). *Right-wing populism in Europe: Politics and discourse.* London: A&C Black.

Wilson, J. (2013). Alternative Media Blocks Globalist Attempt to Launch WW3. Retrieved March 15, 2019, from www.infowars.com/alternative-media-blocks-globalist-attempt-to-launch-ww3/.

Yardi, S., & Boyd, D. (2010). Dynamic debates: An analysis of group polarization over time on twitter. *Bulletin of Science, Technology & Society, 30*(5), 316–327.

Zannettou, S., Bradlyn, B., De Cristofaro, E., Sirivianos, M., Stringhini, G., Kwak, H., & Blackburn, J. (2018). What is gab? A bastion of free speech or an alt-right echo chamber? arXiv preprint arXiv:1802.05287.

Zannettou, S., Caulfield, T., De Cristofaro, E., Kourtelris, N., Leontiadis, I., Sirivianos, M., ... Blackburn, J. (2017). The web centipede. In *Proceedings of the 2017 Internet Measurement Conference on IMC '17.* ACM Press. doi:10.1145/3131365.3131390.

Index

Note: Page numbers followed by "n" denote endnotes.

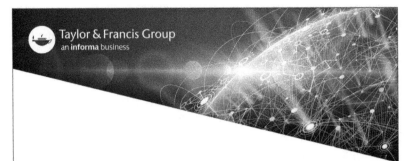